Taking Back
What's Been Stolen

A STOP STEALING Workbook

Elizabeth Corsale, MA, MFT and Samantha Smithstein, Psy.D.
Pathways Institute Press
Pathways Institute for Impulse Control
www.pathwaysinstitute.net

ISBN: 0615813925

This workbook is designed to be used as part of a comprehensive treatment program for people with a compulsive stealing disorder. Group therapy, often in conjunction with individual therapy, is the recommended treatment modality for people who compulsively steal. If expert assistance or counseling is needed, the services of a competent professional should be sought.

For more information on Pathways Institute resources, please go to the website **www.pathwaysinstitute.net,** call **415.267.6916** or email **help@pathwaysinstitute.net** for information on treatment, materials for licensing, workbooks, workshops and training.

This publication is sold with the understanding that the authors and publisher are not engaged in rendering psychological, medical, financial, legal, or other professional services. Any similarity between persons or places in this text and those of any particular reader are purely coincidental.

Pathways Institute Press

Pathways Institute for Impulse Control, A Psychology Corporation
5758 Geary Boulevard #227
San Francisco, CA 94121
www.pathwaysinstitute.net

Contents

Introduction

When I was a kid I used to pray every night for a new bicycle. Then I realized that the Lord doesn't work that way, so I stole one and asked Him to forgive me.
   - **Emo Philips**

Want of money and the distress of a thief can never be alleged as the cause of his thieving, for many honest people endure greater hardships with fortitude. We must therefore seek the cause elsewhere than in want of money, for that is the miser's passion, not the thief's.
   - **William Blake**

The **STOP STEALING WORKBOOK** is the first workbook written for people with compulsive stealing disorders and the therapists with whom they work. Compulsive stealing is commonly referred to as *kleptomania*: the inability to resist the urge to take things that don't belong to you. This book gives individuals suffering from kleptomania and compulsive stealing effective and practical methods to stop their destructive behaviors. It also provides clinicians the diagnostic and treatment tools to effectively help their patients.

Stealing and Society

Stealing has a profound impact on our society. Billions of dollars are lost each year due to theft, lost jobs, and increased fees and prices that are passed on to consumers. And those suffering from compulsive stealing also lose – kleptomaniacs are often deeply ashamed and don't seek treatment. They lose jobs, families, and health because of their inability to resist their impulse to steal. They build long rap sheets of criminal charges and can spend years in prison, destroying their lives and those of their families.

Sadly, in spite of this there has been little research done on compulsive stealing disorders. Stealing has been around as long as we have, and yet we understand little about why people steal. The popular cultural stereotypes of individuals that steal represent two extremes: an anti-social criminal who is selfish, self-motivated, and has no conscience, to a crazy old aunt that everyone in town knows steals everything she gets her hands on, whom the family quietly ignores or repairs the damage she wreaks on the community. People have fixed stereotypes about who steals and why they do it. In reality, this population is diverse: some people steal daily, some go for long periods of time without stealing; some steal only from small retailers, while some steal from big box stores as well as family and friends. The common experience is the inability to resist the urge to steal no matter how frequent or infrequent that urge arises. And it is clear from the occasional news story of a celebrity who has shoplifted that it is not just the poor, but the rich and middle class who also steal.

In addition to a scarcity of research, there is unfortunately very little specialized treatment available to people who steal. Small scale studies have suggested that up to 7% of the population may suffer from kleptomania. (In comparison, Bipolar Disorder is estimated to be 3% of the population). ***But there are only a handful of specialized treatment programs in the entire United States.***

Why This Workbook is Important

This workbook is important because the suffering caused by and experienced from out-of-control stealing behaviors is tremendous. These men and women need help, and this workbook is an important addition to their care and treatment.

This book is based on years of direct clinical experience assessing, diagnosing and treating people who steal. Founded in 1995, our program has worked with hundreds of people helping them gain control over their stealing behaviors (and other addictive, compulsive and impulsive behaviors). And for the past 15 years we have provided individual therapy and groups for people with compulsive stealing problems. With little marketing we have always had a steady stream of referrals – people who have been caught stealing and are desperate to try to change their behavior before it ruins their lives.

As the years have passed, we have also experienced a steady stream of contacts from people who *do not* live in our area or cannot afford our services. From across the United States people who feel out-of-control about their stealing have called or emailed, desperate for help, asking if we know of specialized treatment in their area. Sadly, we've had to tell most of them that we do not know of any. We also get calls from therapists looking for either specialists they can refer clients to, or any training available in their area. Again, there is a scarcity of both available.

Because of this experience, it seemed a natural step to transform our experience and group curriculum into a workbook – thus making our expertise available to a much wider audience.

Who This Book is For

There is a great deal of misunderstanding about kleptomania and patients with compulsive stealing behaviors. All too often people with kleptomania and compulsive stealing issues are never assessed or treated for their stealing behaviors. Those who do seek treatment often arrive in therapy when their criminal records are so dire that they are facing life-altering consequences. And patients who aren't specifically seeking treatment for stealing behaviors rarely disclose they have a problem because the shame is too great. People understandably fear how disclosing their stealing problem may negatively impact others' perception of them.

Most people who steal compulsively are deeply ashamed and know that their stealing is wrong and against social norms and values. Because their behavior conflicts with their values, they often seem to lack self-awareness and self-understanding - they are in deep denial, and don't understand the behavior themselves. So when shoplifters are told to "just stop" or "don't you know the trouble you are causing yourself and your family," it misses the point that they are suffering from an impulse control disorder and these individuals are not in control of their behavior. This is analogous to the alcoholic who cannot have just one glass of wine to relax.

The STOP STEALING WORKBOOK is written for people with kleptomania and compulsive stealing disorders. It is designed to give you effective and practical methods to stop these destructive behaviors. It is a step-by-step approach designed to: 1) educate you about stealing disorders; 2) help you discover the origins of your impulse to steal; 3) learn how to address the issues that arise when you feel the urge to steal; and 4) build a solid relapse prevention plan to stop any future stealing. We also provide you with a program to help decrease the *urge* to steal.

This workbook is also designed to provide clinicians with the diagnostic and treatment tools to effectively help their patients. The most effective use of the workbook would be in conjunction with weekly therapy, where the issues that emerge or difficulties with the material can be addressed in depth. More often than not, we find that underlying issues such as mood disorders, unmet needs, difficulty tolerating emotions, unhealthy relationships, etc., drive stealing behaviors. Often there are other addictive behaviors that need to be addressed as well, such as eating disorders, substance abuse or shopping/spending addiction.

For most people, *stopping* stealing is only the first step. After stopping, the hard work of uncovering the sources of the behaviors and their triggers begins, as well as learning how to prevent relapses and reduce the primary urge to steal. Addressing these issues, one by one, with the help of others such as an experienced therapist, 12-step programs, and often a psychiatrist, nutritionist, or meditation or yoga instructor, is crucial for a successful recovery.

There Is Hope

Gaining control over stealing behaviors is not easy. Alcoholics can avoid going to a bar, but out of necessity we all walk in and out of stores constantly, and so people who compulsively steal are routinely immersed in a world of temptation. People who suffer from disorders related to compulsive stealing often feel helpless over their compulsion and hopeless they can ever stop, even after they have been arrested and face frightening criminal charges, jail time or loss of relationships.

This workbook offers you hope. There is no guarantee that if you complete all of the exercises you will never steal again. In fact, it is not uncommon for relapses to occur, and rather than a failure, a relapse should be considered an opportunity that can provide you with more information about the problem as well as the increased insight needed to prevent future relapse.

That said, this workbook provides you with the accumulated knowledge from our years of experience working with people who steal and what helps them to stop. We highly recommend you take this workbook to a therapist and work through each of the exercises with the help and support of someone who can help you see areas that are difficult for you to see yourself. We believe that if you complete this program in its entirety to the best of your ability, you'll be a lot further along in gaining control over your stealing behavior. We hope that you find it helpful in this regard, and that it helps you to address your underlying issues and needs in a way that is healthier for you *and* society.

Chapter 1
The Stages of Change

Congratulations! If you are on the first chapter of this workbook, you have taken the first steps on the road towards stopping your compulsive stealing behavior.

People seek help for a problem for all sorts of reasons. Sometimes, it's because they are tired of behaving the way they do – they're tired of feeling out-of-control, guilty, ashamed, afraid, compulsive, and are ready to turn over a new leaf. Other times, they're compelled to get help because there have been negative consequences for their behavior – they got caught, got in trouble, or others discovered their behavior. Finally, there are times when they are compelled to get help and make a change, either by court-order, legal directive, or ultimatum from someone important in their life (i.e. "*If you don't get help, I'm leaving*").

Whatever the motivation to get help, change is a step-by-step process that takes time. People enter the process at different points – largely depending on how they got there to begin with – and sometimes move backward briefly before moving forward again. Rather than thinking about them as stages that follow a certain order, they are more like stations that we travel through – and sometimes re-visit – on our way to making a true, lasting change. It can be helpful during the process to be aware of where you are in the change process.

STAGE 1: PRE-CONTEMPLATION or Not Thinking about Changing

In this stage, the individual has not yet identified that there *is* a problem with his or her behavior. Other people are concerned, but either the person does not listen or is not convinced. If there *have been* negative consequences experienced, they have not been negative enough to spur the person to change.

Case Example
Paris, a 22-year-old woman, was recently caught shoplifting at a store. She convinced the store owner not to call the police or file charges, and promised her humiliated and upset mother that

she would never do it again. Her mother, aware that this was not the first time Paris had shoplifted, buys her a workbook to help, and makes an appointment with a therapist. Paris flips through the workbook but doesn't really feel like it applies to her, because she has the problem "under control." She cancels the appointment with the therapist, and continues to shoplift.

STAGE 2: CONTEMPLATION or Considering Change

In this stage, the individual enters into a dialogue or debate about their behavior. She or he vacillates between the idea of changing ("You are right, I do need to change.") versus defending the old behavior ("Everything is under control, I'm fine."). The person may still feel unable to change and that *continuing* the behavior is their only choice. The outcome of this stage tips the individual either on to the next stage of change, or back to the first stage, depending on how they weigh the pros and cons [see Decisional Balance exercise].

Case Example

Mark, a 41-year-old married man with three children, has a harrowing moment while stealing and nearly gets caught. When he gets home, he is still shaken and resolves to get some help. He has resolved to stop stealing many times and yet somehow finds himself doing it again. He has too much to lose. He researches possible treatment programs and writes down some numbers. The next day, he puts off calling, thinking, "I have too much to do. I'll call tomorrow." The numbers get "lost" on his desk until he walks by the store again and remembers the experience. He thinks, "I have got to make those calls! I really don't have this under control." However, as days go by he begins to feel more confident that maybe he DOES have it under control. He feels relieved not to have to figure out a way to pay for treatment and to schedule it into his already busy life.

STAGE 3: PREPARATION or Getting Ready

In this stage, the individual's ambivalence is over, action starts and serious efforts are made to develop strategies to correct behavior. The person "tries out" methods of change (e.g. "white knuckling" it, workbooks, 12-step meetings, therapy). In order for this stage to be successful, the person must identify what, exactly, needs to change. This is obvious on the surface – for example, to *stop* stealing. But most of the time there are deeper issues that need to be identified as well. Some parts of the individual's life may be functioning well, so it's important to identify his or her strengths versus problem areas. This is the stage where the individual needs to fine-tune goals, and those goals should feel achievable and aligned with that person's values.

Case Example

Michelle is a 36-year-old woman with a successful career as a medical assistant. However, she has grown tired of the ups and downs that stealing has created in her life, including tension with her spouse and secrecy from her closest friends, and is resolved to making a change. She has tried "white knuckling" - just stopping on her own and trying to resist the urge - but this has failed her too many times. She attended a few teleconference 12-step meetings and this helped her feel less alone, but it wasn't enough. She feels she wants to stop stealing, but she also wants a more healthy relationship with her spouse and to be more intimate in her friendships. She cannot find a stealing treatment program in her area so she decides to complete the Stop Stealing Workbook while working with a therapist who understands compulsive behaviors.

STAGE 4: ACTION or Making Efforts to Change

Graduation to this stage is measured by observable lifestyle changes; those who know the person intimately would be able to see that change is taking place. The individual has made an investment in a change program and in concrete changes in his or her life. Learning and commitment to change is integrated and is acted on. The person is challenged to abstain from past behaviors and adopt healthy replacements.

Case Example

Maya, a 28-year-old woman, has successfully completed the Stop Stealing Workbook. While completing the workbook she has also been in weekly individual therapy and has brought each of the exercises to her therapist to fully understand and work through each chapter. She has also telephoned in monthly to the 12-step meetings and received regular support on her progress. As a result of her efforts she has been able to refrain from stealing and has also made some changes in regards to her relationships, communication and at her job.

STAGE 5: MAINTENANCE or Sustaining Change

In this stage, the individual has been successful at replacing undesirable behavior with healthy, positive ones. There is acknowledgment of a history of problematic behavior and steps are taken to foster *ongoing* beneficial behaviors – maintenance systems are in place. The person works on preventing relapse and learning from any relapses that may occur so that it doesn't happen again. Support – support group, therapy, supportive people in that person's life – is active and ongoing.

Case Example

Kai, a 53-year-old man, hasn't stolen anything for the past eight months - the longest he has gone without stealing for as long as he can remember. He has a more intimate relationship with his spouse and through the help of a couples' therapist their communication has improved. He also finds himself much less resentful and happier. He's exercising more regularly and his spouse and friends are supportive of the growth and changes he has made. Opening up to them about his problem was frightening and shameful, but having their support has made a huge difference for him. He feels free to take people with him shopping when he is concerned about stealing and that helps him abstain. He's still in weekly individual therapy, and from time to time he references the workbook to refresh his memory regarding key exercises and to make updates.

Exercises

1. From reading the descriptions of each stage above, what stage of change do you feel you are currently in?

2. How do you know you are in that stage? Try to be as honest with yourself as possible.

3. If you are in Pre-Contemplation, what are some of the ways in which you *still justify* your behavior or tell yourself you don't need help?

4. What are some of the aspects of your life that you need to change that you have tried to ignore?

Decisional Balance Exercise

Decisional Balance: An evaluation of the pros and cons of changing to see which way the scales tip – toward changing or not changing – through a ***cost-benefit analysis***.

Directions: Write as many items as you can in each category (a minimum of five of each). Try to be completely honest with yourself about the benefits you get from continuing the behavior (e.g. it feels good in the moment) as well as what the behavior is costing you (e.g. loss of trust of others).

Cost-Benefit Analysis of Changing My Behavior

Negative Consequences (what the behavior is costing me)	**Positive Outcome** (what I get from continuing the behavior)

Chapter 2

Communication Skills

Learning to communicate is one of the cornerstones of getting control over your stealing behavior. While it may not seem directly related to stealing, most people who steal have troubled relationships and difficulty achieving a deep and satisfying intimacy with others. Poor communication is one of the most common reasons for a lack of intimate connection with others – in order to feel connected, we must feel that the other person accurately perceives and understands us, and vice versa. Learning communication skills is one of the keys to more intimate, satisfying relationships, something that will make stealing a thing of the past.

"I" versus "You"

In the absence of emergencies ("Help! I'm drowning!"), communication comes from an inner drive to share one's thoughts or opinion. Typically, the desire is either to share one's inner world, or to offer insight, correction, or make change in another person or event. This second type of drive often results in "you" statements (e.g. "you should listen to her" or "you never do what you say you are going to do"), otherwise known as accusations or commands. Unfortunately, for both speaker and listener, this type of statement is the most challenging statement to hear; at times it is virtually impossible to respond without defensiveness (protecting oneself from perceived attack). Making an "I" statement is a challenge and initially unfamiliar, but it is more honest and yields better results.

Watch out for: "*I* think *you…*" This is a "you" statement in disguise. For example, "I think you should go" is very different from "I would like you to go."

Case Example

Tania, 45-year-old mother of three with a 20-year history of stealing was admitted into our program. During the assessment she used almost exclusively "you statements" which meant she was "other based" and unable to communicate her internal world of thoughts or feelings clearly and accurately to the therapist. One example was while she discussed an argument with her boss immediately prior to her most recent stealing incident, she stated "he made me angry."

*Immediately the therapist noted her use of "you statements" and recommended in her treatment plan that Tania learn to use "I" statements. This patient needed to **own** her experience in order to begin to be reality-oriented, a critical first step in relapse prevention. She needed to understand that she was angry at her boss, that it was her **internal reaction** to their conversation and it was **her experience** of feeling angry that triggered her relapse. In this example we can see the importance of how we are impacted by how we think and speak to ourselves and others.*

Feelings versus thoughts

Similar to the confusion about the "I" versus "you" habit, people often confuse thoughts with feelings. In later chapters, we will delve deeper into identifying feelings, however, it is important to begin to be clear which you are expressing – opinions or feelings. In the absence of political debate, your work is to attempt to express feelings about things and people, rather than thoughts. Expressing thoughts often invites debate, whereas expressing feelings invites intimacy.

Watch out for: "I feel like…" This is most often a thought in disguise. For example "I feel like you don't love me," which is a thought, and very different from "I feel afraid you don't love me," which is a feeling.

Case Example

*Dahlia, a 25-year-old environmental engineer, had a history of shoplifting since she was in high school. When Dahlia first came into therapy she was unable to identify any feelings and when asked would say, "I think I felt sad." She was dissociated from her feelings and her inability to communicate clearly was a clue to early trauma that had occurred and left her defended against feeling anything. Slowly over several years of group and individual therapy she began to feel more connected and safe enough to **feel** her feelings, and she learned how to describe them in her communications.*

Listening

Listening is not nearly as easy as it seems. Most people gather their own thoughts and reactions instead of truly listening to the other person. Most times we don't check to be sure we understood correctly, nor do we try to understand why someone is thinking/feeling that way and then let them know. *Mirroring*, or reflecting back what someone has said in our *own* words and being empathic about what they said, is a way of giving another person the experience of being truly and accurately seen and heard, as well as making sure *we* heard correctly.

Mirroring has two steps:

1. Checking for accuracy: "It sounds like what you are saying is…" During this step, we re-phrase what the person has said in our own words to make sure we understood what they said.

2. Demonstrating understanding: "I understand why you would feel that way because…" During this second important step we *empathize* with their experience and show that we understand it.

Mirroring does not mean that you don't have a right to your own feelings, or that you won't have a turn to express your feelings, or that you agree with what is being said. It simply means that you respect and understand the experience of the other person.

If both people in a discussion are able to use "I" statements, speak about their feelings and mirror each other, most of the work of communication is accomplished and intimacy is achieved. The rest (compromise, decision, etc.) will easily follow.

Communication Example:

Sam, a 23-year-old graduate student, is often in a rush and doesn't think much about kicking off his shoes and leaving them scattered about when he comes into the apartment he shares with his roommates. One day Jonathan enters with a bag full of groceries, doesn't see the shoes, and trips over them, nearly dropping the whole bag. He puts the bag down, takes some deep breaths to calm the adrenalin and anger, and addresses Sam:

Jonathan: Sam, can I talk with you for a moment?

Sam: Sure, just give me a sec. (He finishes what he is doing and comes into the living room.) What's up?

Jonathan: I am really feeling frustrated and angry. I tripped over your shoes on the way into the apartment and nearly lost my bag of groceries.

Sam: I can understand that - you were coming into the apartment with your arms full of food and because my shoes were lying there you tripped and nearly lost the whole bag. I can see how that would be upsetting for you.

Jonathan: Yes. Thank you. Could we find another solution for your shoes?

Sam: Sure. Let's talk about it.

In this example Jonathan asked Sam for a good time to talk when he was ready. He expressed his feelings using "I" statements and in a non-accusatory way. Sam listened non-defensively and mirrored Jonathan's experience. They were able to move swiftly to working on a solution rather than getting in an argument.

Passive/Aggressive/Assertive

Generally, people tend to communicate their anger in one of three ways, without being fully aware much of the time what they are doing.

1. *Passive*: Experiencing an action without responding or initiating an action in return. When someone passively responds to anger, they may feel internal distress but generally don't express it outwardly. They take no action but instead try to "just let it go" and "not rock the boat."

2. *Aggressive*: Behaving in an actively hostile fashion. When someone responds aggressively to anger, they explode. They may yell, slam doors, throw things, or even shove or strike the other person. Their response includes intensity and is confrontational.

3. *Passive-aggressive*: Dodging unpleasantness while avoiding confrontation; also called passive resistance. A passive-aggressive response to anger could include being "too tired" to do the promised chore, or "forgetting" to run the expected errand. It could also include "letting slip" personal information to someone else. Generally the person doesn't ever acknowledge they are angry, but does things that seem "minor" but are very upsetting to the person with whom they are angry.

4. *Assertive*: Behavior that is directed towards claiming one's rights – *without* denying the rights of others. Assertiveness is the most direct and healthy way to express anger. The person is able to express their feelings and experience directly to a person

with whom they are angry, while still respecting that person. It is a way of ultimately furthering understanding and even intimacy.

Exercises

1. Do you typically use "I" or "you" statements?

2. Under what circumstances are you most likely to use one or the other?

3. How aware are you of your feelings (versus thoughts)?

4. How often do you speak about your feelings?

5. What do you find difficult about speaking about feelings and using "I" statements?

6. Do you feel vulnerable talking about your feelings and using "I" statements? What feels vulnerable about it?

7. Try mirroring someone this week. What was it like for you?

8. What result did you get from mirroring?

9. Try listening to someone and not respond. What was it like for you?

10. What feelings or thoughts came up?

11. Do you tend to be more passive, aggressive, passive-aggressive or assertive with respect to anger?

12. If you are not assertive, why do you think that is?

13. If you know someone who you would consider assertive, give an example of how they show their assertiveness.

14. What would it be like for you to be that way?

Chapter 3

Impulse Control Disorders

An Overview

According to the *Diagnostic and Statistical Manual of Mental Disorders* (DSM IV-TR), an impulse control disorder is characterized by "the inability to resist a drive, impulse or temptation to perform a harmful act to the person or others." It also describes how the individual feels an increase of tension and/or arousal prior to following through with the act and then experiencing gratification, pleasure or relief at the time of committing the act. Often the relief is short-lived; and while many people feel guilt, shame or regret, others may not feel these at all.

Thoughts

There are many characteristics of impulse control disorders. Often one is preoccupied or obsessed with thoughts involving impulses, cravings and acting out behaviors. Preoccupation can include elaborate fantasies involving the gratification of the impulse. Thoughts about impulsive behavior are often distorted and not based in reality, such as, "I won't get caught," "It doesn't hurt anyone when I steal," and so on.

Case Example

Mary, 35-year-old, had been shoplifting since she was a teenager. She would often spot an item and then feel a strong urge to steal the item in spite of having the money to purchase the item. When she was prevented from stealing the item for some reason, she would obsess and plot her next move to successfully steal. She would spend hours going over the details of when she could go back, how to get the item and how not to get caught.

Tolerance and Loss of Control

People with impulse control disorders characteristically have an increase of tolerance to the behavior. This means that they must *increase* the amount and frequency of the behavior in order to achieve the desired excitement or pleasure. This behavior leads to loss of control over one's self, life and relationships. People often make attempts to stop the behavior, but these attempts usually don't succeed in bringing about stopping stealing over the long-term. As the behavior continues, people can experience further loss of control, loss of careers, divorce, decline in physical health and psychological disorders such as anxiety and depression.

Case Example

Eileen, 40-year-old divorced mother of two, had been in and out of jail four times in the past decade due to her shoplifting. Eileen recognized that she had a problem years ago, but hoped it would just go away. She tried to stop, but when things in her life became stressful she would find herself going to stores and stealing. She knew she didn't want to go back to jail, but even the thought of jail wouldn't deter her because, as she would say, "I don't remember anything about jail when I am about to steal something."

Negative consequences only worked briefly after being caught. Eileen said that she finally really woke up and knew she had a significant problem when she walked into a home improvement store and walked out lugging and dragging an 8x10 rolled up carpet. No one caught her, no one stopped her! She told her therapy group that it terrified her because she had never before been so bold and brazen in her stealing! She feared what she would do next. Gone were the days of hiding something in her coat pocket or purse. She had graduated to riskier and riskier behaviors.

Shame and Secrecy

Shame and secrecy remain the characteristic hallmarks of impulse control disorders, and particularly kleptomania. These two aspects and others often make the individual who suffers from an impulse control disorder experience intense feelings of isolation and self-loathing. Impulse control disorders are frequently not well understood by the suffering individual or by their family and friends.

Many people who have come to our program have never discussed their impulsive stealing behaviors with anyone close to them. You may wonder how this can be, but people will concoct elaborate lies and financial schemes to cover the problems their stealing has created. And often they won't tell loved ones about their problems until it is unavoidable, such as a repeat offense with a guaranteed jail sentence. Most people hide their stealing in order to avoid their deep and painful feelings of shame.

Case Example

Lou is a 46- year-old woman with multiple stealing offenses. She called the program after having been arrested and charged in order to set up an appointment. She admitted she had been shoplifting for years and that no one ever knew about it. She had been arrested a few times, but because she had significant means of her own she was able to retain a top-notch San Francisco lawyer who could help her deal with her legal problems. But she said this time was different: her lawyer said he could help, but the best he could do was get her "house arrest" for three months because of her prior arrests. Lou was desperate because she was going to have to tell her husband of 25 years of her behavior.

What Causes Impulse Disorders?

An understandable question is: what causes an impulse control disorder? There is currently no conclusive answer, however, there has been research and hopefully with new brain imaging technology, genetic research and DNA mapping we will learn even more about the etiology and neurological underpinnings of impulse control disorders. There is a high co-morbidity (dual disorders) between impulse control disorders and affective mood disorders (anxiety, depression, substance abuse). This research suggests that mood disorders may underlie impulse control disorders. We see impulse control disorders in people who have sustained traumatic brain injuries and those with substance abuse disorders. We do know that impulse control disorders are made worse by stress and even worse yet by overwhelming stress. If one experiences a rise in stress either internally or externally, one's ability to resist an impulse is decreased. Identification and then the reduction of stress is an essential element in the treatment of people with impulse control disorders.

There appears to be differences in levels of severity amongst people with impulse control disorders. It is common for impulse control disorders to become more severe over time if left untreated, or if they do not increase in severity, they will have a long-term corrosive impact in the individual's health and relationships.

One of the main reasons it's so difficult to change an impulse control disorder is dopamine. Brain research shows that both addictive drugs and highly pleasurable or intense experiences – such as a life or death thrill, a crime, or stealing – trigger the release of the brain chemical dopamine, which in turn creates a reward circuit in the brain. This circuit registers that intense experience as "important" and creates lasting memories of it as a pleasurable experience. Dopamine changes the brain on a cellular level, commanding the brain to "do that pleasurable thing again," which heightens the possibility of relapse even long after the behavior (or drug) has stopped. Dopamine also helps to explain why intense experiences can be just as addictive as drugs, and why compulsive behavior is about powerful memories, and recovery is a slow process in which the influence of those memories is diminished.

Additional research on addiction indicates that dopamine is not just a messenger that dictates what feels good; it also tells the brain what is important and what to pay attention to in order to survive. The more powerful the experience, the stronger the message is to the brain to repeat the activity for survival.

Additionally, those who have fewer things in their lives that capture their interest and attention are more vulnerable to those things that may give them a rush and alert the brain in a powerful way. This research on dopamine goes a long way in explaining how someone can become addicted to something that can become so destructive and detrimental in their lives and the lives of those they love.

We do know from research that psychological treatment, behavioral changes, social and family support and for some, psychiatric medication create the best recovery outcomes for people suffering with impulse control disorders.

Exercises

1. Do you feel a build-up of tension that is relieved when you act out an impulsive behavior?

2. Can you describe your experience of impulsive urges?

3. Do you feel the impulsive urge in your body, feelings and/or mind?

4. Have you tried unsuccessfully to stop an impulsive behavior, and if so, what happened?

5. Have you tried and *successfully* stopped an impulsive behavior, and if so, how did you accomplish this?

6. Does your mood change when you try to resist the impulse? How?

7. At that time, do you feel more tension or less?

Chapter 4

Kleptomania/Compulsive Stealing

Compulsive stealing is commonly referred to as kleptomania. Kleptomania is the inability to resist the urge to take things that don't belong to you. Often the individual feels compelled to think and scheme about places and objects they want to go and steal. Fighting the urge to steal can be a daily, weekly or monthly battleground. Each person's stealing behavior has unique characteristics.

Kleptomania was first observed in the 1800's by French psychiatrists and has a two-hundred-year history of coming in and out of psychiatric medical and legal fashion. In our program we have seen that kleptomania or compulsive stealing afflicts men and women alike, crosses all socio-economic, racial, ethnic and educational lines. *What kleptomaniacs share are the urges to take things that do not belong to them.* Typically the phrases "It doesn't belong to me" and, "I'm hurting others" are alien. And the stealing cycle leads nowhere but to depression, anxiety, criminal records and destroyed relationships.

The most current Kleptomania diagnosis is found in the *Diagnostic and Statistical Manual of Mental Disorders* (DSM IV-TR). Listed below are the five current criteria for a diagnosis of Kleptomania:

- Recurring failure to resist the impulse to steal objects not needed for personal use or monetary value.
- Increasing sense of tension immediately before committing the theft.
- Pleasure, gratification, or relief at the time of committing the theft.
- The stealing is not committed to express anger or vengeance and is not in response to a delusion or hallucination.
- The stealing is not better accounted for by Conduct Disorder, a Manic Episode, or Antisocial Personality Disorder.
- *It is important to note that not all people who suffer from kleptomania/compulsive stealing fit these diagnostic criteria.*

Case Example

Joey is a 35-year-old single man with a history of stealing and boosting (selling the items he stole). He was in and out of jail for drugs, physical assault and stealing. He was not remorseful and felt psychological treatment was a waste of time. He was only in group because his attorney said it would help his current pending criminal case. Joey did not meet the criteria for kleptomania or an impulse disorder. He had a criminal lifestyle and anti-social personality features.

Case Example

Barbara was a 52-year-old single woman with a 45-year history of shoplifting. She began shoplifting as a child not long after her parents divorced. Barbara had never been arrested and prosecuted. She contacted our program because she said she could no longer bear the guilt and shame of her stealing. During the assessment, she described being unable to go to stores without feeling the urge to take something, even though she could afford all the things she stole. She appeared deeply remorseful and afraid because she was admitting that her life and her stealing behavior were out of control. She described three incidents over the years of being caught but not being arrested, and cried when she said that each time she vowed she would never steal again. But, even the shame of being caught was unable to change her impulsive behavior.

Additional Characteristics of Compulsive Stealing

Review and answer the following questions in order to understand if your stealing behavior is out of control and compulsive:

Inability to Control Behavior: Are you unable to control your stealing? In other words, you tell yourself to stop stealing but you find yourself doing it again. Do you make deals with yourself and try to make bargains about your behavior? Have you repeatedly stopped and then started stealing again?

Irrational Behavior and Thoughts: Do you repeat your stealing behavior again and again, even though it puts you at risk, is dangerous, harmful and it is not rational and doesn't make sense?

Behavior That Interferes with Your Life: Do you continue to steal despite the serious negative consequences on your life/health? Have you been caught or arrested? Have family members found out about your behavior and asked you to stop?

Values: Do you find yourself behaving in ways that are outside of your value system? In other words, stealing even though it is contrary to your beliefs, values, attitudes and spiritual practices? Are you ashamed of your stealing?

Case Example

Sarah, a 30-year-old single woman, had a history of shoplifting, switching price tags and stealing things from work. Sarah described elaborate fantasy plans of running away if stopped while shoplifting or turning and fighting the person who confronted her. Her group members were concerned about her irrational behavior and thoughts and her unwillingness to stop stealing. One group member confronted her when there was an article in the local paper describing the shooting of a shoplifter fleeing a store by a security guard. Sadly, the shoplifter in the article died. The group member told Sarah they were afraid she was going to get hurt, or worse. Sarah was finally able to see that out of control stealing behaviors and her fantasies were distorted and irrational. She was completely out of control and needed to accept her problem and accept help to stop her stealing.

The Nature of Compulsive Stealing

Why do we steal?

It makes us *feel better right now*. Is this true for you?

It is *compensatory*; meaning that it is an attempt to fill a psychological/emotional emptiness or a way to avoid painful or uncomfortable feelings.

Why does stealing become compulsive? It feels good, just fantasizing about it feels good, it meets many emotional needs. It is highly sensory and has a physiological effect on both brain and body. It's readily available and has an effect psychologically.

DIG: the Desire for Immediate Gratification

Cravings and *urges* are what you feel when you have a compulsion or addiction. A craving is a desire for the pleasure or relief – a discharge of anxiety – that you get from the compulsion, in this case stealing. Cravings can start either from a bad feeling from which you want to escape, or from something that reminds you of some pleasure you had in the past. An urge is an intention to do a specific thing (steal) to satisfy that craving. Taken together, the craving and the urge are known as the **DIG – Desire for Immediate Gratification**. The DIG can drive you to find a way to satisfy your desire without giving thought to the consequences – thus, you DIG yourself into another hole, in spite of not wanting to end up there.

DIG in action:

1. **Bad feeling/reminder**-- this is an emotion or trigger that is difficult to manage and makes you more likely to think about stealing.

2. **Craving**-- you begin to feel a yearning to steal -- a desire for the pleasure or relief that stealing may bring.

3. **Fantasy** -- you begin to think about stealing. Fantasy can be a quick, fleeting moment or a prolonged full-fledged fantasy, but either way it is the moment when you imagine that stealing is going to help you feel better.

4. **Urge**-- you have the intention to steal.

5. **Distorted thinking**-- these are thoughts you have to rationalize your behavior (e.g. "Just one more time," "Just a small thing no one will notice," "They make so much money it won't cause them any problems," etc.).

6. **Planning**-- elaborate planning or split-second planning; the plan is hatched for how to make the stealing happen.

7. **Seemingly Unimportant Decision**-- for example, just running into the store to grab some milk you need or you "remember" you need some socks as your favorite socks have holes. These are the little decisions that seem so innocuous and harmless, but really are the decisions that walk you right up to stealing again.

8. **High Risk Situation**-- you are in the store and an item to steal is within your grasp.

Mapping out the DIG is the first step in creating a Relapse Prevention Plan -- it gives you a step-by-step map of how relapse happens so that you can begin to think about how to prevent it. We will be talking more about relapse prevention throughout the workbook and how to stop stealing. But the DIG is crucial for you to see how you get to the point where you are stealing. Each point along the way represents a fork in the road. If/when it can be recognized, the movement towards stealing can be stopped, and instead a different choice can be made. Often people feel as if they don't know how they found themselves suddenly stealing. Mapping out DIG helps to see the steps you actually take to get to the point where you are back in that hole again.

IMPORTANT NOTE about cravings and urges:

Cravings and urges most typically follow the shape of a bell. In other words, they start out weak and grow in intensity until they peak and feel overwhelming. The peak is usually when people relapse. A helpful aid in *preventing* relapse can be the awareness that after the peak, the urge will recede again. In other words, if you can just breathe through the most intense desire to act out and reassure yourself it will pass – and not last forever – then the intensity will lesson and it will get easier. This experience builds trust in the outcome of the *next* time, and that the *intensity* of the peak will lesson as well.

Exercises

1. Evaluate your behavior: What patterns does your stealing behavior take? Think of rate, stealing rituals, amount and frequency, the emotions you feel – before, during and after you steal – places you steal, and objects you steal.

2. Do you ever buy something and then steal something else to "even" things out?

3. Do you steal when you are angry or lonely?

4. Look at the four characteristics of compulsive stealing and the diagnosis of kleptomania provided above and explain how each applies to you. If there are characteristics of *your* stealing that are not mentioned, write them down. Don't worry if your stealing behavior doesn't appear to follow all the criteria and characteristics above.

Give an example of how DIG typically looks in your life: what would the eight steps towards the stealing behavior look like for you?

1. **Bad feeling/reminder**: These are emotions or triggers that are difficult to manage and make you more likely to think about stealing.

2. **Craving**: You begin to feel a yearning to steal -- a desire for the pleasure or relief that stealing may bring.

3. **Fantasy**: You begin to think about stealing. Fantasy can be a quick, fleeting moment or prolonged full-fledged fantasy, but either way it is the moment when you imagine that stealing is going to help you feel better.

4. **Urge**: You are motivated to steal.

5. **Distorted thinking**: These are the thoughts you have to rationalize your behavior (e.g. "Just one more time," "Just a small thing no one will notice," "They make so much money it won't cause them any problems," etc.).

6. **Planning**: Elaborate planning or split-second planning; the plan is hatched of how to make the stealing happen.

7. **Seemingly Unimportant Decision**: For example, just running into the store to grab some milk you need, or you "remember" you need some socks, as your favorite socks have holes. These are the little decisions that seem so innocuous and harmless, but really are the decisions that lead you to stealing again.

8. **High Risk Situation**: You are in the store and an item to steal is within your grasp.

Chapter 5

Stinkin' Thinkin':

Cognitive Distortions and Thinking Errors

When people are engaging in self-destructive, impulsive behaviors such as stealing, the underlying thoughts that support the behavior are composed of thinking errors. Thinking errors are irrational and distorted thoughts that deny, exaggerate, and/or minimize reality and allow you to justify stealing. An important part of treatment and recovery is to analyze your thoughts through therapy, cognitive exercises and reality testing. At times you will also need the help of others to determine when, how, whether and why your thoughts are distorted. Without this work it's too easy to allow yourself to justify stealing again.

People who have been stealing for a long time are usually very conflicted about their behavior. And they've employed sophisticated psychological defenses in order to "not think" about their actions and the impact they have on themselves and others. Very often people start out in recovery not knowing or being unable to answer many of the questions loved ones and therapists ask them about their stealing. The exercises below are not meant to shame you, but rather to get you thinking about *your* thinking, which is a critical skill to learn as you progress in your recovery.

Case Example

DeeDee, a 30-year-old single woman with a 15-year-history of stealing, came to treatment to try to stop. She wondered what was wrong with her: she felt stealing was wrong, experienced feelings of self-loathing after stealing and getting away with it, and felt terrified another arrest would ruin her life, and knew stealing was wrong. Still, she had been unable to stop on her own. She talked extensively about her "crazy" thoughts. She described thoughts like, "it doesn't hurt anyone," "I am a horrible person," "I won't get caught," "I can talk my way out of being arrested if I get caught," "I will run out the security exits if I get caught." She believed the thoughts when she thought them, but when confronted by her therapist, she could see they were distortions and not based in reality.

DeeDee saw that she would slip in and out of believing her distortions. And slowly over time, she began to understand that these were not "real thoughts," but rather defensive statements or denial reactions to her serious problem that had to be addressed if she wanted to stop this self-defeating and destructive compulsion. She began to see the difference between real thoughts about stealing, and defenses that only appeared to be thoughts.

Exercise I - Listening to your thoughts

To learn about *how* you think, and what your thoughts are, you have to first start listening to them. Only then will you be able to question if they are reality-based. For the next five days, try to listen to your thoughts about stealing. Every time you have a thought about stealing, write them down – unedited. List at least 10 examples of thoughts you tell yourself about your stealing, such as, "It won't hurt anyone." You'll use some of these thoughts in the following exercises.

Exercise II- Different Kinds of Thought Patterns

In order to understand if your thoughts contain distortions, you need to learn about different kinds of characteristics that define cognitive distortions and thinking errors. Below is a list of common types of cognitive distortions. Review the list, and after each description of a thought distortion, see if you can find three examples of this type of thinking *in your own mind*. Try to locate examples related to stealing and other problem areas in your life. You can use the thoughts from the list you generated from Exercise I, or any others that occur to you as you look at the list.

After making the list of thought patterns and examples, try to identify the feeling that underlies each one. Write that under it.

Minimizing: Making things less significant than their likely impact.
Example:
Thought: *"This store makes a lot of money. They won't even notice if I take this single shirt."*
Feeling: *Self-righteous. Justified.*

My thoughts:

My feelings:

Black and white thinking: Seeing people, places and things in all-or-nothing terms.

Example:

Thought: *"I am a terrible and horrible person for stealing." "There is nothing good about me."*

Feeling: *Self-loathing, shame; I'm all bad. Paralyzed.*

My thoughts:

My feelings:

Exaggeration or over-generalization: Taking a single event or experience and generalizing it as how things will always be.

Example:

Thought: *"I am so good at stealing, I won't ever get caught."*

Feeling: *Powerful; invincible.*

My thoughts:

My feelings:

Filtering: Picking one detail and dwelling only on that detail despite the full experience.

Example:

Thought: *"I don't cause much social harm with my stealing because, I only steal from big box stores and not small 'mom and pop' shops."*

Feeling: *Righteous, dismissive.*

My thoughts:

My feelings:

Disqualifying the positive: Rejecting positive experiences by telling yourself, "They don't count," thus maintaining a negative belief that is contradicted by your every day experience.

Example:

Thought: *"I can't believe I stole something after two months of not stealing anything. I should just give up on recovery."*

Feeling: Hopeless.

My thoughts:

My feelings:

Jumping to conclusions: Believing that a situation will end unpleasantly even though there are no supporting facts to indicate such an outcome.

Example:

Thought: *"Why should I seek help for my shoplifting? No one will ever understand me and worse, they will judge me as bad."*

Feeling: *Stuck.*

My thoughts:

My feelings:

Catastrophizing: Expecting the absolute worst and embellishing it further.

Example:

Thought: *"My family will never forgive me for having a stealing history, no matter how hard I work at recovery."*

Feeling: *Ashamed, paralyzed, hopeless.*

My thoughts:

My feelings:

Emotional reasoning: Assuming your negative, unpleasant and positive emotions are the full or true reflection of reality.

Example:

Thought: *"If I don't steal new things to wear, no one will want to be my friend, and they will judge me as 'un-cool'."*

Feeling: Insecure, afraid.

My thoughts:

My feelings:

Should statements: "I *should* do this or that." Using these types of statements indicate self-criticism and likely patterns of guilt when you are unable to meet the expectations of what *you* think you "*should.*"

Example:

Thought: *"I should stop wanting and desiring things and then I won't steal anymore."*

Feeling: Guilty, deprived.

My thoughts:

My feelings:

Personalizing: An inability to separate events from yourself in your thinking.

Example:

Thought: *"That store clerk was so rude to me after I waited in line for ten minutes. I deserved to take that coat for their imposition."*

Feeling: *Victimized, entitled.*

My thoughts:

My feelings:

Exercise III– Reality-Testing

When you are stealing something, the situation may feel complicated, but in reality it is simple and clear: you are taking something that does not belong to you. Reality-testing is what you use to find out if your thinking is grounded in reality, or if you're just confusing things to avoid thinking about it or to justify the behavior.

How do you test your thoughts for reality? It is actually simple: **identify the stealing-related thought**, such as "It doesn't hurt anyone," **and then list as many of the self-defeating or destructive consequences of that behavior**. Consequences such as "It does hurt my partner when I am absent and involved in stealing" or, "If enough people steal it hurts the store and people lose their jobs." Focus on what is actually true. In the section below you will be asked to practice a reality-testing exercise.

The following is a list of common distorted thoughts that people have in relation to their stealing behavior. Use any of these that apply to you as well as all of the examples you listed above. When you complete the list of thoughts, take time to write the negative consequences of that thought. Then write what the thought would be if it was a reality-based thought instead - in other words, what the *truth* is.

I won't get caught.

I deserve it.

I can talk my way out of it, *if* I get caught.

It doesn't hurt anyone.

It doesn't hurt my relationship.

The store won't miss it.

There won't be any consequences.

Am I living a lie?

It impacts my work.

It impacts how I feel about myself.

I am saving money.

I can buy something so the store clerks won't suspect.

I want to get caught.

I want to be punished.

I am bad.

It takes time away from things or people I truly love.

Distorted Thoughts (what I tell myself that allows me to steal)	**Reality-Based Thoughts** (what is actually true)

Hidden Meaning

We can learn much by studying the content of our distorted thoughts. Often hidden in distorted thoughts are feelings, fantasies, wishes and painful memories. It may be that you have suffered, experienced trauma or have underlying mood issues that the distorted thoughts are trying to tell you about – in an unconscious way – much like dreams. Therefore, identifying the *irrational* thoughts you have about your stealing can help you to begin to understand what is hidden in their meaning and help explain what you need to learn about yourself and areas you may need to work on to heal. This additional information will help you, and your therapist, understand the psychological and emotional work you need to do in order to support and speed your recovery.

Example:

Thought*: "I deserve to do or to have what I want."*

Unmet need*: "I've had many unmet needs in the past. This strong feeling of "deserving" is actually about a painful "deficit" or host of "unmet needs" I'm trying to fill."*

Case Example

Franklin, a 42-year-old history professor, came to therapy for his stealing when he was caught stealing and sentenced to treatment by a community court. Franklin had been in therapy before and found it quite helpful. Originally he entered therapy as a young man to deal with anxiety related to a learning disability he had as a child. During that early therapy he never spoke of his stealing because he felt too ashamed. Now, Franklin was ready to work at stopping the stealing because he didn't want to experience that kind of terror and shame ever again. He looked closely at his thoughts prior to and during a stealing episode and realized they seemed to be connected to feelings of neglect, and as a result feeling like he deserved something special. He came to understand that stealing was his way of dealing with the painful feelings of never getting the help he needed as a child and that he'd had to find his way through the educational system all by himself. Although that in itself was an exceptional achievement, he was left feeling deeply insecure. His stealing was a way of "acting-out" the painful experience of always being on his own.

Exercise

It's difficult to find hidden meaning on your own, but even if you don't have a therapist, it is still worth the effort. Take 10 of your thoughts that you wrote in previous exercises and see if you can find the hidden meaning in each.

Chapter 6

Getting a Handle on Feelings:

Emotional Instability vs. Emotional Regulation

Emotional Instability

One of the hallmarks of individuals with compulsive stealing is emotional confusion, instability and sometimes volatility. People who steal often have difficulty with feelings: difficulty identifying and naming feelings and "numbing-out," or emotionally withdrawing from oneself or others. Most people who struggle with stealing have a strong belief that they will always feel the same, and their feelings will never change. You may blame your feelings on others and communicate these beliefs with defensive communication, such as "You made me feel...." You may have difficulty communicating feelings using non-defensive "I statements." Often people who steal allow difficult feelings such as anger to escalate into rage and then justify inappropriate communication, aggression and violence. Or you may find it difficult to tolerate your feelings and "numb-out" (or dissociate).

Acting-out by stealing is often an attempt to avoid, escape or change your feeling-state or mood. You may steal or plan to steal as a way to get rid of anger or anxiety. You may have difficulty recognizing your stress levels and how to make changes to reduce that stress. You may have difficulty understanding the value of the information that feelings bring, or how to use that information for constructive communication and behaviors. You may have difficulty being able to empathize and understand others' feelings. You likely find it very difficult to figure out what you are feeling when faced with someone else's feelings – you may become confused about who is feeling what. You have difficulty valuing all your feelings, even the most powerful feelings such as sadness, fear, anger and excitement. And often, you may find yourself trying to create a particular feeling and trying to hold onto it, unable to recognize when you're emotionally flooded or overwhelmed by feelings, and unable to seek relational support.

Case Example

Eric, a 23-year-old graphic designer, entered treatment to deal with his compulsive stealing. During the first meeting, he talked about all the relationship problems that he had with family members, friends and the opposite sex. He described being in emotional upheaval frequently and when the chaos subsided, he would feel anxious. He had great difficulty communicating his needs, desires, boundaries, and expressing his feelings. He shared that his "go to" emotion was always anger. He said he was in a vicious cycle of getting angry, anxious, sullen, and then feeling guilty.

Characteristics of Emotional Regulation

Emotional stability is something for which we all constantly strive. And we find we have better days, weeks and months once we have stopped stealing and committed to our recovery. But it's a one-day-at-a-time process, because even when we've gained a lot of sobriety from our stealing, life is still happening to you. We will be given wonderful days, good days, OK days, lousy days and some really terrible days. There will be losses and gains. So what does coping look like when we have a healthy relationship with our emotions and feelings?

You will know when you are able to feel, identify and name your feelings when you are able to take the time to sit and feel *what* you are feeling and *where* you are feeling it in your body. You will be able to recognize that ***thoughts are not feelings***, but that thoughts occur in our mind. Thoughts can generate feelings, and feelings nearly always generate thoughts, but they are not the same thing. You will understand the always-changing nature of feelings, and not try to hold onto a particular feeling or strive for a feeling state.

You'll have improved communication skills and be able to communicate your feelings by using non-defensive "I statements."

You'll be able to measure your stress levels and make behavioral changes in order to reduce that stress. You'll understand the important information that feelings bring, and use that information to guide constructive communication and behaviors. You'll develop empathy, compassion and understanding about others' feelings. You'll value **all** of your feelings -- even the most difficult feelings such as sadness, fear, anger and excitement -- and not want to escape them. You'll recognize when you're emotionally flooded or overwhelmed by feelings, and seek relational support from others. You'll have an emotional support system. And you *won't* be afraid of anger and know how to communicate that anger in ways that de-escalate rage and avoid aggressive and violent communication and behaviors

Emotional regulation is crucial for preventing relapse. Because the feelings you have difficulty tolerating are often those that lead you back to unwanted behaviors, you feel the urge to escape the feelings that you can't tolerate.

Case Example

Pearl was a 30-year-old professional woman who entered therapy to deal with her stealing behaviors. She described feeling nothing for herself or others and that stealing gave her a "high," which she preferred to the feeling of numbness. She spent several years in group therapy, individual therapy and received psychiatric medication for depression. In therapy she worked on relapse prevention and the impact of her psychological and mood-related problems in her relationship with herself and others. She left treatment in touch with and feeling her feelings; she could feel her anger, happiness, joy, disappointment and a whole range of other emotions. Pearl told her therapist that she was using the information that her feelings gave her to guide her choices and now felt like she was finally alive!

A Note on Eating Disorders

Often, people who use stealing as a way to try to deal with overwhelming feelings use food in a similar way. When you experience anger, shame, sadness, longing or loneliness, and feel out of control or overwhelmed, you might find yourself bingeing on certain foods. Afterwards, you might feel overwhelming shame and a profound need to purge, or rid yourself, of the food. This eating disorder, known as *bulimia*, must also be addressed in learning how to tolerate and experience emotions. And you may need to work specifically on the eating disorder with a therapist and a nutritionist.

Exercises

1. Are you able to identify all your feelings? If not all, which ones? In other words, which feeling do you feel you never have or can't relate to? Use the provided list of feeling words (p.49).

2. What feelings are feelings you *can* feel, name and feel okay feeling? Why?

3. What feelings can you feel, identify, but don't feel okay feeling? Why?

4. Review the paragraph on emotional instability. See how many of the characteristics with which you identify. List them, and give examples.

5. Are you able to use "I statements" when discussing your feelings? If not, take some time to write about why you are unable to use "I statements" and what might happen if you started using "I statements."

6. How do you feel and think about your feelings? Do you value your feelings? Do you think of feelings as useful information, or a hindrance?

7. Do you recognize, consider and try to empathize with other's feelings?

8. Do you ever blame others for what you feel?

Feeling Words

Pleasant Feelings

OPEN	HAPPY	ALIVE	GOOD
understanding	great	playful	calm
confident	gay	courageous	peaceful
reliable	joyous	energetic	at ease
easy	lucky	liberated	comfortable
amazed	fortunate	optimistic	pleased
free	delighted	provocative	encouraged
sympathetic	overjoyed	impulsive	clever
interested	gleeful	free	surprised
satisfied	thankful	frisky	content
receptive	important	animated	quiet
accepting	festive	spirited	certain
kind	ecstatic	thrilled	relaxed
	satisfied	wonderful	serene
	glad		free and easy
	cheerful		bright
	sunny		blessed
	merry		reassured
	elated		
	jubilant		

LOVE	INTERESTED	POSITIVE	STRONG
loving	concerned	eager	impulsive
considerate	affected	keen	free
affectionate	fascinated	earnest	sure
sensitive	intrigued	intent	certain

tender	absorbed	anxious	rebellious
devoted	inquisitive	inspired	unique
attracted	nosy	determined	dynamic
passionate	snoopy	excited	tenacious
admiration	engrossed	enthusiastic	hardy
warm	curious	bold	secure
touched		brave	
sympathy		daring	
close		challenged	
loved		optimistic	
comforted		re-enforced	
drawn toward		confident	
		hopeful	

Difficult/Unpleasant Feelings

ANGRY	DEPRESSED	CONFUSED	HELPLESS
irritated	lousy	upset	incapable
enraged	disappointed	doubtful	alone
hostile	discouraged	uncertain	paralyzed
insulting	ashamed	indecisive	fatigued
sore	powerless	perplexed	useless
annoyed	diminished	embarrassed	inferior
upset	guilty	hesitant	vulnerable
hateful	dissatisfied	shy	empty
unpleasant	miserable	stupefied	forced
offensive	detestable	disillusioned	hesitant
bitter	repugnant	unbelieving	despair
aggressive	despicable	skeptical	frustrated
resentful	disgusting	distrustful	distressed

inflamed	abominable	misgiving	woeful
provoked	terrible	lost	pathetic
incensed	in despair	unsure	tragic
infuriated	sulky	uneasy	in a stew
indignant	bad	pessimistic	dominated
worked up	a sense of loss	tense	
boiling			
fuming			
indignant			

INDIFFERENT	**AFRAID**	**HURT**	**SAD**
insensitive	fearful	crushed	tearful
dull	terrified	tormented	sorrowful
nonchalant	suspicious	deprived	pained
neutral	anxious	pained	grief
reserved	alarmed	tortured	anguish
weary	panic	dejected	desolate
bored	nervous	rejected	desperate
preoccupied	scared	injured	pessimistic
cold	worried	offended	unhappy
disinterested	frightened	afflicted	lonely
lifeless	timid	aching	grieved
	shaky	victimized	mournful
	restless	heartbroken	dismayed
	doubtful	agonized	
	threatened	appalled	
	cowardly	humiliated	
	quaking	wronged	
	menaced	alienated	
	wary		

Chapter 6.2

Anger

Anger is one of the most basic human emotions: it is a physical and mental response to a current perceived threat or a reaction due to harm done in the past. Anger is a feeling that troubles many people with impulse control disorders. One of the most important yet difficult tasks is to identify the underlying source of your anger. Usually, anger is about feeling something is unfair and feeling powerless to make it fair. Rage is extreme, long-lasting anger. Typically, the things that make people feel this way are the things they can't control or change: they feel powerless, and hence this feels intolerable.

Anger can put you at risk of acting impulsively and stealing. When you are angry, it often feels like taking action (stealing) can help to regain a sense of power and control. Faced with the same situation, some people will feel angry and others will not. Some will show their anger, in a variety of ways, while others will keep their anger to themselves. It's crucial for you to discover what situations make you feel angry, and then how you tend to feel it and express it so that it will not trigger you to steal.

It's important to note that *anger isn't always negative*. It can be a force for good, for positive change. And what sometimes feels like anger is often not really anger, but may be the way that shame, hurt, fear, sadness, disappointment or insecurity is being felt or expressed.

How Anger is Experienced in our Bodies

Anger gets the mind and body ready for action. It arouses the nervous system, increasing the heart rate, blood pressure, blood flow to muscles, blood sugar level and sweating. It also sharpens the senses and increases the production of adrenaline, a hormone produced at times of stress.

Anger Influences our Thinking

When we're first faced with a threat, anger helps us to quickly translate complex information into simple terms, such as "right" or "wrong." This can be useful in an emergency so that we don't waste valuable time weighing information that doesn't instantly affect our safety or well-being. However, this can also mean that in *non*-emergency situations, we act before we've considered what else is relevant, and may have made an irrational decision about how to behave. When anger gets in the way of rational thinking, we may give in to the urge to act aggressively. It may be that when we are angry, we need to pause, take more time to look at the situation and weigh all of our options in order to find the best way to act.

Ways Anger Often Gets Expressed

- *Verbally*: shouting, threatening, use of dramatic words, bombarding someone with hostile questions or exaggerating the impact on them of someone else's action.
- *Physically*: throwing things, slamming doors, hitting something, ripping something up, shoving someone or hitting them.
- *Acting the Martyr*: making others feel guilty and playing on that guilt.
- *Criticism*: developing a cynical attitude and criticizing everything but not addressing problems directly or constructively.
- *Indirectly*: acting in ways to seek revenge or to anger the other person, without directly expressing anger.
- *Internalizing or Resentment*: seething inside, not expressing outwardly, manifesting physical ailments, holding on to anger, inflicting self-harm.

Most often how we express (or don't express) anger is from modeling – from, or in reaction to – our family of origin.

Anger Management

Anger management is the process of learning to understand your anger and how to control it.

It consists of:

1. Awareness of anger.
2. Taking responsibility for anger.
3. Changing destructive or unhealthy patterns of expressing anger into healthy communication.

Passive/Aggressive/Assertive

Generally, people tend to communicate their anger in one of three ways, without being fully aware much of the time that is what they are doing.

1. *Passive*: A passive approach to anger is when you receive or are subjected to an action without responding or initiating an action in return. When someone passively responds to anger, they may feel internal distress, but generally don't express it outwardly. They take no action, but instead try to "just let it go" and "not rock the boat."

2. *Aggressive*: An aggressive approach to anger is when you behave in an actively hostile fashion. When someone responds aggressively to anger, they explode. They may yell, slam doors, throw things or even shove or strike another person. Their response includes intensity and is confrontational in style.

3. *Passive-aggressive*: A passive aggressive approach is about dodging unpleasantness and avoiding confrontation by employing passive *resistance*. A passive-aggressive response to anger could include being "too tired" to do the promised chore, or "forgetting" to run the expected errand. It could also include "letting slip" personal information to someone else. Generally the person doesn't ever acknowledge they are angry, but does things that seem "minor," but are very upsetting to the person with whom they are angry.

4. *Assertive*: Assertiveness is an expression of anger that is directed towards claiming your rights, but without denying the rights of others. Assertiveness is *the most direct and healthy way* to express anger. The person is able to express their feelings and experience directly to the person with whom they are angry, while still respecting the other person. It is a way of ultimately furthering understanding and even intimacy.

Exercises to Help with Anger

1. Keep an anger log for a week. Make a list of each event that made you angry. Write down the thoughts you had at the time, the level of anger (rate it "low," 1, "moderate," 2, or "high," 3). Note what your behavior was in response, and what a more effective alternate behavior might have been.

2. Practice taking a "time-out." The key to healthy anger expression can simply be the difference between placing time between your experience and your expression of your feelings. Notice the signs of anger building. Take some time and engage in a physical activity. Think about your anger – notice if there may be other feelings underlying the anger, such as hurt, and then return to discuss it, if necessary. Time-outs should include, at minimum, a slow count to 20. It *should not* include: impulsive behavior, substance use or abuse or anything dangerous.

3. Imagine what your calmest friend would say to you, and give yourself that same advice.

4. Practice good communication skills.

Chapter 7
Stopping the Behavior:

Behavioral Regulation

While the *reasons* for your stealing may be a combination of thoughts, feelings, conditioning, wounding, mood, etc., at the heart of the matter is a *behavior that needs to be changed.* Behavioral change requires internal change as well as lifestyle change and attention to concrete action. While it may feel less shameful to believe that stealing is "spontaneous" or "spur of the moment" rather than coming from planning, this is rarely the case (and ultimately more worrisome). In other words, we may tell ourselves that stealing "just happens" unexpectedly, and that just may be what it feels like sometimes. But in truth, it is exceedingly rare that someone has that level of complete impulsiveness. It is much more likely that instead you just need to become conscious of the lead-up to stealing. Often there is elaborate scheming beforehand, both fantasy and behavior of which you may or may not be aware.

Case Example

    Jill was the daughter of a wealthy rancher in Texas. She had struck out on her own and become a school teacher. Although she came from wealth and attended the best schools, she lived just on her teacher salary.

    Every year at Christmas time, Jill would agonize about all the gifts she felt she needed to get for her relatives and friends in order to impress them. She would tell herself that only expensive things would do and she should try a little harder to save up money to pay for gifts. Jill would spend a great deal of time worrying about all the special gifts she needed to get for the various family members – yet she never took any action.

    As Christmas would draw near and she was out of time to make gifts – and didn't have the money to buy gifts – she would head out into the holiday rush and steal gifts. Last year she was arrested and when talking to her therapist stated, "I can't believe how stupid and lazy I am." This example shows a pattern of seemingly unimportant decisions that result in the patient stealing gifts for family members. The patient was unable to plan, set boundaries or accept reality. Only when she was arrested and no longer in denial did she reach out for support to get the help she needed to stop stealing.

The Cycle: Identifying the Cycle of Stealing

1. **Lifestyle Risk Factors**: A lifestyle that doesn't satisfy ones needs may lead a person to attempt to meet those needs in unhealthy ways (i.e. through stealing). It's important to spend time figuring out the underlying feelings and needs that drive you to steal.

2. **Triggers**: A trigger is anything that brings up thoughts or feelings about wanting to steal. A trigger can be *external* to yourself - in other words a situation you find yourself in that makes you want to steal. Or it can be an *internal* experience - a feeling inside you - or both. What sparks the urge to steal?

3. **Fantasy and Desire**: Typically when you are triggered, you begin to have thoughts about stealing. This can be a brief, fleeting, flash fantasy to steal, or it can be an elaborate fantasy about where, when and how you might do it.

4. **Plan** (and **Seemingly Unimportant Decision**): These are the little plans that get hatched that lead to stealing. And even when they're not full plans to steal, they can walk you up to the edge of the behavior. For example: spending time with someone who may encourage or enable you to steal, or planning a quick errand to stop by a store on the way home from work.

5. **High Risk Situation**: These are situations that make you feel most out-of-control, and are the greatest triggers of your stealing behavior.

6. **Loss of Control:** This is that point at which you "give up" and just steal something. Up to this point, you haven't stolen anything, and even though it may feel "inevitable," you still have a choice not to steal.

7. **Action:** You steal something.

8. **Evaluation**: These are the things you tell yourself after what just happened. These evaluations can range from, "I did it again," to "No matter what happens I will always keep stealing," to "That wasn't my fault - if he hadn't done that I wouldn't have stolen anything," to "I'm on the road to recovery and just relapsed – and I need to learn how to make sure this doesn't happen again."

Additional Notes

Identifying healthy urges or desires are the keys to this exercise, because unmet needs, either from the past or present, can start the Cycle moving forward. Later in the workbook we'll focus more on what those needs are and how they might be met in healthy ways. Behavioral regulation is related to making a commitment to change.

Case Example

Mark had been in group therapy for several years working on stopping his stealing behavior. He was doing well and had only one relapse in the first nine months of therapy. He began to see that in addition to his impulsive stealing, he had difficulty in his relationship with his wife. He had a hard time establishing boundaries regarding the family budget, specifically around expenses for their three children. He felt that the number of each child's expensive after-school activities was beyond their means and creating financial stress. His wife ignored his concerns and wouldn't negotiate or work towards finding a solution.

Mark realized he had a lot of resentment and anger over the situation. He realized he didn't have the communication skills to speak to his wife without yelling and getting in an argument. Mark realized that in the past he frequently stole things after he would argue with his wife over their finances. Mark asked his therapist to work with him on communication and dealing with his anger in a constructive way. Once he learned to communicate with his wife – without getting angry and yelling – she was far more receptive to talking and working out financial solutions.

Exercises

1. Now is the time to really start defining exactly what the behavior(s) is/are that you need to stop doing, and from these behaviors, defining exactly what "abstinence" looks like. Some behaviors may be obvious (e.g. stop taking things out of a store without paying for them) but there may be others that are more subtle and need to really be defined (e.g. stop taking pens home from work unless I return them the next day). What are all of your behaviors and how do you define them? Make a list and be as specific as possible.

2. Fill out the Cycle of Stealing for yourself as completely as you can. List as many things in each category as you can. Pay close attention to the thoughts you have during each phase/step, and write examples from each step.

My Cycle of Stealing

 1. **Lifestyle Risk Factors**:

 2. **Triggers**:

 3. **Fantasy and Desire**:

4. **Plan** (and **Seemingly Unimportant Decision**):

5. **High Risk Situation**:

6. **Loss of Control:**

7. **Evaluation**:

3. What does a complete Cycle tell you about any lifestyle changes you need to make or things you need to avoid?

4. Are you willing to make the necessary commitments? Why or why not?

5. What does your Evaluation Stage look like? What do you *usually* tell yourself afterwards?

6. How does your evaluation affect what happens in the future?

Chapter 8

The Buck Stops Here:

Responsibility & Accountability

Denial: Definition and Role

Making any change, including stopping stealing behaviors, requires admitting you have a problem. This can be one of the most difficult tasks a person faces.

What is denial? Denial is a *defense mechanism* – a way of avoiding realities, or facts that make us uncomfortable when the reality is too painful, shameful, embarrassing or threatening. In other words, it's a way to defend ourselves from the pain of reality. Denial, therefore by its nature, makes people defensive and prohibits change and progress in treatment.

While denial causes many problems, it can also help you from getting in trouble. Because giving up denial can feel very dangerous and frightening – and it can mean facing consequences – coming out of denial can represent a tug-of-war: with reasons for honesty (making a change for the better) versus reasons for denial (avoiding painful reality). It is truly an internal tug-of-war that only each individual can decide which side wins.

Types of Denial

There are five types of denial:

1. **Denial of the Facts:** This type is when you deny what you have actually done – by either minimizing or lying. (e.g. "I didn't steal that," or "I haven't stolen in a long time.")

2. **Denial of Intent:** This is when you deny that you set out to steal, that it was your intention to do so. (e.g. "I was high," or "I didn't know what I was doing," or "It was spontaneous," or "I didn't mean to.")

3. **Denial of Impact:** This is when you don't admit to yourself or others that the stealing had a negative impact on someone else. (e.g. "They're a big company, they won't even

notice," or "It wasn't really hurting anyone (self or other)," or "No one will even notice.")

4. **Denial of Responsibility**: This is when you blame someone or something else for your stealing, rather than taking personal responsibility. (e.g. "It wasn't my fault," or "I was driven to do it by someone else.")

5. **Denial of the Need for Treatment**: This is when you tell yourself or others that you don't need help or treatment to stop stealing, that you can handle it on your own, even when you have been unable to do so. (e.g. "I don't need anyone's help," or "It won't happen again," or "I can control myself.")

Case Example

Martha made a frantic call to our program to discuss treatment for her 35-year-old daughter. When the therapist returned Martha's call, Martha shared that her daughter had been arrested and convicted three times in the past seven years, and that she found out the previous night that her daughter had been arrested again at the local Safeway. Martha knew her daughter shoplifted on a regular basis because she always had new things that Martha knew she couldn't afford. Martha said that she needed to set up an appointment for the very next day and that she would be coming in with her daughter in order to get her the help she needed. The therapist asked Martha to have her daughter contact her directly in order to speak with her about the program and confirm the appointment. Martha said that she would ask her daughter to call right away. Sadly, Martha's daughter never called. Her daughter was still in denial and not yet ready to admit she needed treatment.

Accountability

What does it mean to be "accountable?" The dictionary defines accountability as: *an obligation or willingness to accept responsibility for one's actions* (Webster).

Responsibility can be shared. In other words, there can be several people who are responsible for a task or for making things happen. But *accountability is not shared*: it's really about taking full responsibility for your actions. (i.e. "The Buck Stops Here," Harry S. Truman). Accountability is ultimately the key to growth, progress in treatment and healing. Accountability is part of preventing relapse – it's about being grounded in the reality of your life, your situation, and taking full responsibility for it.

Case Example

*Alana came to the assessment appointment expressing deep remorse about her stealing behavior. She described herself as a selfish person who did bad things, with stealing being the worst of her actions. Five weeks into the group therapy process she continued to berate herself as a bad, selfish, foolish person. The therapist began to understand and then shared with her that although it **seemed** like she was taking "full" responsibility, her shame and self-criticism was getting in the way of her really taking responsibility. The therapist asked Alana to go back to the first exercise and get really honest about what stage of change she was in regarding her stealing. In doing so, Alana realized that although she felt very remorseful about her stealing, she still wasn't really sure she wanted to stop.*

Case Example

George decided after he completed our program that he was going to go back to school and become a counselor. Years before, he had dropped out of the counseling program at the college he was attending. He now realized that not only had he stopped stealing and gained a life free from his impulse disorder, but he wanted to help others do the same. He continued to stay in therapy, participated in 12-step programs and kept his commitment to staying "sober" from stealing. He's now training in another state and planning to work with individuals with compulsive stealing behaviors and kleptomania. George was becoming a "model" for others.

The Six Elements of Accountability

Accountability means taking full and complete responsibility for your behavior:

1. *Admission:* admitting the behavior(s) AND the extent of your problem.
2. *Acceptance of Consequences:* not feeling victimized and understanding that the consequences are a result of your own actions.
3. *Restitution:* taking action to try to right the wrong.
4. *Supervision:* acknowledging that you may need the help of others not to relapse, including being supervised in some way.

5. ***Prevention***: recognizing your triggers and cycles and being open to the feedback of others.

6. ***Modeling***: being an example to others.

Exercises

1. Re-read the five types of denial. How have you employed each of these types? Write examples of each and how it applies to you:

1. **Denial of the Facts:**

2. **Denial of Intent:**

3. **Denial of Impact:**

4. **Denial of Responsibility**:

5. **Denial of the Need for Treatment**:

2. Now re-read the six elements of accountability. Again, write how each one applies to you.

    1. *Admission*:

    2. *Acceptance of Consequences*:

    3. *Restitution*:

    4. *Supervision*:

    5. *Prevention*:

    6. *Modeling*:

Chapter 9
Secrets & Shame

"Shame" versus "Guilt"

John Bradshaw defined the difference between guilt and shame this way: Guilt says "**I have done** something bad;" whereas Shame says "I **AM** bad." In other words, guilt is accountability and the awareness that we have done something wrong and wish to behave differently in the future. Shame is related to self-esteem and can be paralyzing. It can also lead to minimizing, cognitive distortions and relapse.

Stealing is often accompanied by guilt, but also by shame. Often shame can be traced back to messages you received at a very young age, yet *still* influence your feelings, thinking and behavior.

How does shame lead to relapse?

Self-statements are the statements we make when we are talking to ourselves inside of our head. Self-statements that are *shame*-based (I am worthless, I am powerless, I am not as good as others, I will fail) lead to shameful feelings. These shameful feelings often lead back to behaviors we are trying to avoid (such as stealing). This is either because we're trying to avoid the resulting shame or as a self-fulfilling prophesy – I am bad so I might as well behave badly.

Secrets

Most frequently, stealing not only brings on shame, but creates a life of duplicity (secrets). Lying, or keeping secrets, can include lies about thoughts, feelings, fantasies and behaviors. Sometimes the "double life" we lead started at a young age, and has shaped choices and behaviors since then.

Keeping secrets can be a way to avoid shame and/or consequences, but it often exacts a heavy toll and can ultimately lead to greater consequences. Getting honest with oneself and others can be terrifying – but also liberating.

Getting honest is crucial for change. It changes your relationship to stealing, and causes you to integrate your behavior into "real life." Making a commitment to honesty is an important part of the healing process and making a lasting change.

Case Example

*Pat was a 40-year-old woman referred by her attorney to our program. When she came to her assessment appointment, she was unable to look at the therapist through much of the appointment. She kept her head down, spoke very softly and wept. She said she was deeply ashamed of herself and her stealing behavior. She knew it was wrong to steal, but there were times when she couldn't control her behaviors. When she discussed being out of control she wept deeply. She said no one in her life knew about her stealing except her attorney and that it was so painful and humiliating that **anyone** knew. She imagined that he and the therapist were judging her as a terrible person and that they were probably disgusted by her. Pat, like many people who steal, was experiencing shame. She moved past "I do bad things," and into "I am a bad person."*

*It took many months of therapy for her to begin to understand she wasn't **all** bad; that yes, her impulsive stealing harmed others, but she had many fine qualities and attributes. Over time she was able to open up little by little and tell the therapist about being sexually assaulted as a child, and not being able to talk to anyone about it because the perpetrator threatened to harm other family members. She learned that she had been exposed to overwhelming stress, that her stealing was in part an attempt to self-sooth and lift her from the deep depression she had struggled with for years. It can be paralyzing for individuals with impulsive/compulsive stealing to only see themselves as **all** bad. And it can get in the way of their work in beginning to identify triggers, trauma, stress and seemingly unimportant decisions that make-up their impulsive cycle of stealing behaviors. Over time Pat was able to accept her illness, accept the trauma, get additional help from psychiatric medication to treat her depression and stop stealing on a daily basis.*

Exercises

1. Do you feel you suffer more from guilt or shame?

2. When did your shame start? Describe the shame-based thoughts that you have. Give examples.

3. How does your shame lead to stealing behavior?

4. When did you start keeping secrets, and what about?

5. What do you lie about (or avoid talking about), and why?

6. How do you benefit from lying?

7. What is the cost to you/your relationships by lying? Be as specific as possible.

Chapter 10

What Lies Beneath:

The Psychodynamics of Your Behavior

What is the unconscious?

The unconscious is a mental process that operates outside of the awareness of the conscious mind. In other words, it's the part of us that thinks and motivates us to behave in certain ways without us being aware of it.

The unconscious mind is the source of our dreams. It also contains memories that we may no longer be able to access or that took place very early in our development.

The unconscious has a powerful influence in our life and can be involved in all kinds of decisions that we think of as conscious, such as who we marry and what we do for a living.

Characteristics of the unconscious mind

If the unconscious mind operates *outside* of our awareness, how do we recognize it when it is at work? Here are some clues:

1. When you have feelings that you don't understand (feelings that don't match up with the situation). Or when you should be feeling something, but instead feel nothing at all.
2. When you feel scared or agitated, but don't understand why.
3. When you are drawn to something that you normally would not be interested in, or might even be repulsed by.
4. When you can't remember something that you think you should (repression).
5. When you're afraid of something, but there doesn't seem to be any reason for the fear – you have no memory of prior negative exposure (unconscious phobia).
6. When you accidentally say something that reveals something about yourself ("Freudian slip").

7. When you gain understanding from the content of your dreams (the royal road to the unconscious).

8. When you gain insight from the content of your daydreams or fantasies.

9. When you find yourself re-creating a traumatic experience.

10. When you find yourself having escape fantasies.

11. When you forget something obvious.

12. When you get caught because of "doing something stupid." Sometimes this can be a way that your unconscious is crying out for help or intervention. The conscious part of you does not want to get caught, but the unconscious part of you causes you to do something that makes it easy for you to get caught.

Case Example

Barb, a 29-year-old woman, was self-referred to our program because she was caught stealing at her gym. She often snuck into peoples' lockers and took nonsensical things. She took socks, t-shirts, things she didn't need, want or could easily afford, and often tossed the things out shortly after taking them. She couldn't understand this urge and felt out of control. She began working in individual and group therapy to stop the behavior. After a time in therapy, she realized this behavior had started when she was 16-years-old and was sent away to boarding school. She'd been adopted at birth and when she was eight, her adopted parents divorced and she stayed to live with her mother. She remembered that as a young child, she would often take things out of her mother's purse when her mother was on the phone, distracted or engaged in work. Her mother would find the missing items in Barb's room, scold her, and then, feeling guilty, would spend a little time with her. Her mom was a busy executive, working long hours, often traveling, and Barb came to understand that she felt she wasn't her mother's top priority.

*When Barb was at boarding school and caught stealing the first time, the school contacted her mother. Her mother rushed upstate to see her and they met with the school officials, then spending a long weekend together. After her mother left, Barb felt that her mother really **did** care for her and that she would "drop" everything in a time of crisis. Soon after the first event, the old feelings of being neglected, abandoned and longing for her mother's attention began to reappear, and so did her stealing. Barb worked long and hard in therapy and finally realized she had deep feelings of insecurity due to the absence of a consistent relationship with* *her mother. Over time she was able to feel and work through all of her feelings of anger, resentment, longing and grief with her mother.*

The unconscious and compulsive stealing

Now that we've defined the unconscious, what does it have to do with compulsive stealing?

Unconscious or repressed emotion can have a direct impact on your impulse to steal. For example, when you repress emotion that needs to be expressed, sometimes that emotion will find a way to express itself anyway: through an impulsive action like stealing. For example, when you feel anger but push it down rather than expressing it, you may find yourself stealing as a way to release that anger.

Also, trauma and traumatic relationships can drive your impulse to steal. Deeply-rooted, early memory and trauma can be part of the cause of your compulsive stealing. Accessing the past and healing it frees you from its power. By integrating it into the present, you can choose your own relationship to it rather than having it "run" you. If you have been unable to process and work-through trauma, it takes psychic energy to repress the memories and feelings. But these experiences *need* to be worked-through and often the urge to steal is an expression of that need. It can be a cry for help from the unconscious.

Sometimes the stories you have created for yourself – about you – promote cognitive distortions and thinking errors as your mind is forced to distort itself in order to hold on to those stories in spite of reality. Also, the unconscious can generate circumstances that begin your journey of living in reality and recovery; for example, if you "forget" to hide an item you have stolen so that another person discovers it.

In order to access the unconscious – in a conscious way – we need to begin deconstructing the thoughts, feelings, Freudian slips and concrete behaviors associated with your stealing, digging deep. It's very difficult to do this work on your own, because you need to learn how to access "pathways" to your unconscious mind. Work with a therapist can often help in this regard.

Unconscious desires and compulsive stealing

The following are a list of examples of desires that may be unconsciously acted-out when you steal:

- Wishing to be "caught in the act" of stealing, in order to get help, have limits and hand-over control.
- An unconscious cry for help.
- Confusing selfishness with long-lost childhood unmet needs; feeling like "I deserve it," rather than understanding there is a longing that can't be met that way.
- Escape fantasies (stealing as a means to "get away").
- Control fantasies (stealing as a way to feel in control).
- Avoidance of intimacy.
- Confusion about real intimacy vs. immediate gratification (feels good right now versus feels good in a deeper way, longer term).
- Wishing to avoid reality and until now, being pretty successful at it.
- Denial of painful loss.
- Avoidance of the lifelong reality of loss.
- Avoidance of attachment and closeness.
- Wishing to get rid of pain.
- Seeking revenge.
- Seeking attention or love.
- Avoiding fear, pain, sadness and loneliness.

Re-creating loss, unresolved early trauma and compulsive stealing

Compulsive stealing is about repeating the same unhealthy behaviors over and over despite the negative consequences. Sometimes this is a way of re-creating past trauma, only this time with the unconscious wish to master the trauma and have it come out differently. Stealing can also symbolize a refusal to accept the reality of the trauma.

Compulsive stealing can create a false sense of accomplishment. This can come from the manic day-to-day nature of running your life, rather than acknowledging your compulsive stealing is running you.

Addictive thinking, compulsive stealing and the unconscious

Addictive thinking is concrete and very different from symbolic/creative thinking. Concrete thinking becomes a block against real thinking. For example: I am upset at my partner so I go to the store and steal (concrete) rather than thinking about the problem with the partner and coming up with solutions (symbolic/creative) to work through the problem.

People who steal compulsively create and use their "addict mind." When someone is using their "addict mind," they are often dissociated and their life looks out-of-control. The "addict mind" causes significant problems with relating to others and to you, and makes it difficult to feel close to others. This is due, in part, to an inability to empathize and sympathize with others. It can also entail difficulty with setting boundaries with others.

The "addict mind" entails self-deception and often a lack of fulfilling responsibilities. This can take the form of: not showing up for your family, showing up for your family or friend but being internally absent and preoccupied, and/or always being late and not understanding why.

Key language in locating unconscious desires

How do we know when unconscious desires, wishes or messages are being enacted? The following are a list of thoughts or statements to watch out for that may be indications:

- I don't know (but I should).
- I never thought about that.
- I have to have it no matter what.
- I don't remember (but I should).
- I don't know what I feel.
- I "think" when asked how I feel.
- I "feel" when asked what I am thinking.
- I forgot.
- I can't remember.
- A dream that you can't shake the next day.
- A movie that sticks with you.

- Song lyrics that you can't get out of your head.

- It was almost like I was possessed by someone else when I did it.

- I feel so anxious/angry/agitated/etc. and I have no idea why.

- I can't help it.

- I know I shouldn't, but I can't help it.

- Words just pop out of your mouth before you can think about it.

Exercises

1. How do you feel about the idea of the unconscious mind being a part of your mind that operates outside of your normal waking consciousness?

2. Have you had encounters with your unconscious mind? Freudian slips? Forgetting? Getting caught at something that shook you up and made you take a closer look at yourself? If so, give examples.

3. What actions do you take to avoid thinking about things?

4. What fantasies are present in your life now? New job, new relationship, desire to escape or move? What is driving the fantasies and are they connected to your stealing? If so how?

5. Can you identify any past trauma or unhealthy relationship patterns that your stealing is recreating?

6. Ponder the unconscious wishes/desires that are part of your stealing. Did you ever secretly want to get caught? Did you get caught how and why? Did you leave things out for your partner, friends or family to find?

7. Have you ever felt that your compulsive stealing was not just a physiological phenomenon, but that it was trying to tell you something or has hidden meaning about your past? If that is true, what might the message be?

Chapter 11
Money & Things:
What to do with the stuff now that you are in recovery?

The things themselves

Now that you are in recovery you may be asking yourself: what do I do with the things I've stolen? The most important first step in dealing with stolen items is to begin honestly talking about the items with your group and therapist. Often the objects have psychological and emotional meaning. We know that often objects from childhood have unique meaning – as young children we often imbue an object with special meaning, and we call that object a "transitional object." It might be a special teddy bear that the child needs to go to bed at night, or to take with them to the babysitter's house. This can be just as true for adults. Objects can hold memories, reminders and even comfort when we are scared, need reassurance and comfort. Stolen objects almost always have meaning attached to them, and it's important to question and ponder the meaning in order to make it conscious. So it can be difficult to make a clear decision about just what to do with the items you've stolen until you gain a clear understanding about the meaning you've attached to them.

Sometimes people find that the things they've stolen trigger thoughts about stealing again, as they remind you of your stealing behavior. You may feel attached to the stolen items and the items may still have meaning or psychological significance, such as security or safety. Seeing the stolen objects may make you feel good about yourself, or the opposite – they may bring you shame or negative self-feelings. People who steal often have fantasies about the stolen objects and feel they need to hang on to them, while others feel they want to give them away.

What to do with the things

An important part of the recovery process is to be honest with yourself about living with stolen items and the thoughts and feelings they bring up. It's important to really evaluate whether or not you feel you can be honest and live with integrity if you continue to live with stolen items.

You may decide that you want to get rid of all of the stolen items. It is important to take the time to work through all the feelings about what living without stolen items means and all the fear and anxiety that will come up if you have to replace items with purchased items. You need to be real with yourself and find out if you can afford to replace everything at once or will it be an on-going process? Do you feel upset, afraid or angry when you read this page and even think about getting rid of the stolen items?

Figuring out what to do with the things you have stolen is an important part of preventing future relapse; it's a part of becoming clear about your stealing and changing your relationship with the objects you steal. Part of how your will gain this clarity is through awareness about your thoughts, feelings and motives about the stolen items. *The more you become aware of the power the objects have over you the more power YOU will have over the behavior.*

Money & Finances

Money and finances are a part of everyone's life and everyone has a relationship to money, and your relationship to money is dynamic and often changing. Money can often cause a great deal of joy, fear and stress for people, and is often especially complicated for shoplifters and those who steal. People who compulsively steal need to begin a new relationship to money as they learn how to not steal – you now have to learn to tolerate paying for everything.

As you make changes – by no longer stealing – you'll be in reality about what you truly want and need. You may or may not be able to afford some things you want or need, and you'll need to work through the thoughts and feelings you experience when this happens. You may also have feelings of deprivation or loss to deal with in your therapy or with a trusted friend. Try not to judge yourself about wanting or needing things. You'll learn to delay gratification and create a reality-based budget that will relieve financial stress, and to do that you may have to revisit your work and career. You may decide to change jobs or go back to school and gain more skills to reach a higher income. This can often feel bad or frustrating at first, but later it might motivate change. It can be very painful to discover that for years your stealing behavior has delayed or "arrested" your own ambition and your ability to make significant professional/career contributions to society. Now that you are in recovery, it is empowering to know you can work and live within your means.

Answering the following questions will give you a better sense of what role money plays in your life, and what you need to do in terms of that relationship. Answering the questions may make you feel anxious or sad. Write about the feelings that come up during each section.

How do you feel about money?

- Does it make you anxious or afraid?

- Do you feel secure about your finances?

- Do your feelings about money impact your stealing/shoplifting?

- Do you express your feelings about money with your family & friends?

- Does your stealing create an emotional fantasy of abundance and security?

- Do you feel resentful of others because of money?

- What were the messages and feelings about money expressed in your family of origin?

- How do you feel about paying for things you use to steal?

Working on Your Relationship to Money

- Do you know what you spend?

- Do you make a budget?

- Do you understand your finances?

- Do you have financial goals that you plan and achieve?

- Was money something openly discussed in your family or was it secretive?

- Does thinking about money go in and out of your conscious mind and life planning?

- Are you impulsive around money? Do you spend more than you earn?

- Do you get into debt in self-destructive ways?

- Do you resent spending money? Why?

- How much stress does money cause in your life?

- Do you and your partner argue over money?

- Do you and your partner deal with money similarly or differently? How?

- How do you plan to pay for everything you formerly stole?

Your Financial History & Future

- Often people who steal have complicated issues related to money. How have you handled your money in the past?

- What changes (if any) do you feel you need or want to make?

- If stealing has been a part of your financial plan, then you will need to begin to look at spending in a new way. Answering these questions may help:
  - What is it you need?

  - What is it you want?

- How has stealing impacted your ability to earn money?

Hoarding

Hoarding is the excessive acquisition of items that make your life unmanageable. Often when patients begin to talk about the items they steal and getting rid of those items, the issue of compulsive hoarding emerges. Sometimes this is when patients begin to understand that they have a *cluster* of addictions, and this can be overwhelming.

Hoarding behavior is often messy and fills one's home with unmanageable clutter that makes daily life activities extremely difficult or impossible. But sometimes hoarding behavior can be organized and free from clutter. When hoarding behavior is free from clutter, it can be harder to identify. One way to identify hoarding is to take stock of the number of similar items you have. For example: do you have 40 pairs of black pants? Do you have hundreds of collectibles, neatly organized in your home?

Think about and then talk to your therapist and group about the "things"" and "amounts" of stolen items in your home. Do you feel that having dozens and dozens of bottles of shampoo makes you feel safe? Do you feel panic or extreme anxiety when the discussion about cleaning, clearing or getting rid of your things takes place?

Diana, a 50-year-old woman, entered our program on her own. Shortly before enrolling in our program, she was stopped at a local upscale food store with stolen items in her bag. The store security decided not to call the police or press charges, but asked her to stop coming into the store. She was deeply grateful that she was not arrested and felt it was a wake-up call. Diana often talked about her anxiety about getting low on staples and food items. She stocked her house with hundreds of rolls of toilet paper, bars of soap, cleaning products and more. And when her supplies began to run low – perhaps down to 75 bars of soap – she would go out and shoplift more. She was deeply anxious about loss and wanted to insulate herself from that anxiety; she never wanted to feel close to running out. Over time, the fear increased along with her hoarding and stealing, so that she stocked literally thousands of things in order to keep her anxiety at bay. Diana began to understand that the cycle of stealing and hoarding was not treating her anxiety. And slowly over time, she became willing to consider and then try psychiatric medication to treat her anxiety, and she continued in treatment to work through the psychological and emotional fears of loss.

Exercises

1. Do you feel attached to the stolen items? How?

2. What meaning do you place on the objects themselves? Do they have psychological significance? Do they represent security or safety?

3. Do the objects make you feel good or bad about yourself? How?

4. Are there any fantasies you have about the objects?

5. Do you feel you need to hang onto the items?

6. Do you feel you need to give them away?

7. Do you feel you can be honest and live with integrity if you live with stolen items?

8. If yes, what are you thinking and feeling about why? If no, what are you thinking and feeling about why?

Chapter 12

Healthy Lifestyle:

The foundation of your new life

Identifying Uncomfortable Feelings

Typically, stealing – or the urge to steal – is preceded by unpleasant emotions or feelings. These feelings can be very difficult to identify, because they're often uncomfortable, so we make intense efforts to avoid them. In other words, we habitually act – steal – before we're even aware of having a feeling so we can avoid having the feeling.

One of the most effective ways to become aware of the feelings is to try to postpone acting when you feel the urge. Use that time to write or sit and be aware of any feelings that are there as long as possible. This can give you a chance to discover from what you are running.

- Be aware that feelings are often experienced as bodily sensations. This can give you clues that you're having a feeling – and what that feeling is.
- Be aware of how cravings and urges can be confused with true desires or needs. This can be quite confusing in the beginning as you try to sort out what you truly need versus what you *think* you need in any given moment.

Identifying Unmet Needs

Compulsive behaviors such as stealing are often *compensatory*, meaning that the urge to steal is fueled by an attempt to meet an unmet need. These unmet needs get *transferred* to the behavior; so behavior is simply a "stand in" or substitute for temporarily getting those needs met.

Of course, the feeling that the need is actually getting met quickly wears-off, and the behavior must be repeated to regain that feeling. This is because the true, deeper needs do not get met, and often there isn't even awareness of them.

One of the most effective ways to become aware of these needs is to identify the feelings *directly* after stealing or when fantasizing about it. Often mixed in with the shame, guilt and self-judgment you might feel, there are positive feelings related to the original need. These feelings could be an experience of power or sensuality, feeling nurtured, a satisfaction of revenge, or others. Another effective way to become aware of the needs is when the urge to steal arises, to pause and think about what happened in the moments *before* you had that urge (or even earlier in the day or week).

Case Example

Juanita, a 26-year-old woman, was self-referred to our program. Although young, she had a lengthy history of impulsive stealing behaviors. When she arrived at her first appointment, the therapist noted that Juanita appeared extremely depressed but very receptive to suggestions and willing to consider all of the treatment plan recommendations. These included: a psychiatric medication referral, recommendation to attend a 12-step program to deal with self/family addiction issues, and weekly individual and group therapy. Over the next 6 months Juanita's depression improved greatly and she regularly attended her meetings and therapy. After 12 months, she had a new job that she liked, and had started dating someone special. Juanita remained in therapy for several years and each year notable progress was made. She was sober in her stealing behavior, no longer depressed, and living a fulfilling life.

Healthy Behavior Replacement

Healthy behavior replacement is one of the cornerstones to change. As feelings are increasingly tolerated and healed, and as unmet needs get met in a healthy way, the desire to steal will lessen -- stealing was, after all, a poor substitute. But, since we don't always know what else to do, discovering a new way can take some time.

Exercises

1. Spend the week trying to tolerate the urge to steal. Write about what you are feeling in the moments those urges comes up.

2. Try to identify unmet needs you're trying to fulfill. Write down as many as come up, and as far-fetched as they may seem.

3. Now look at the first two lists. Place the feelings and unmet needs in one column. And in a second column, write a list of ways you might get those needs met, or how you might cope with those feelings in a healthy way. *Stay as far away as possible from "**should.**" Instead, try to stay with what would really work for you and what is truly appealing.*

Feelings and Unmet Needs	Other Ways I Could Get The Need Met or Help Myself with the Feelings

4. Create a list, as long as possible, of behaviors that you have found to be fun and/or fulfilling in the past.

5. Create a list, as long as possible, of behaviors that you imagined would be fun but never tried.

Chapter 13

Impact on Others:

How do I make it right?

Overview

Stealing affects not only the person who steals, but others in their lives. People often tell themselves that they are "not hurting anyone" by stealing - this is a cognitive distortion/ thinking error. Stealing *always* affects others. These affects can range from loss of trust, loss of intimacy, job loss, loss of role models for children, and negative impacts on victims and society.

Acknowledging the suffering of others as a result of our stealing is incredibly hard. But it's necessary for apologizing, making restitution and healing. And it's the beginning of compassion – which has great personal value.

Restorative Justice

Restorative Justice is based on the Native American principle that criminal behaviors are offenses against human relationships and that after these behaviors are committed, there are both dangers and opportunities:

- The *danger* is that everyone emerges further alienated, more damaged, disrespected, disempowered, feeling less safe and less cooperative.
- The *opportunity* is that injustice is recognized, equality is restored and the future is clarified. So that participants are safer, more respectful, and more empowered and cooperative with each other and society.

Restorative justice is a process designed to try to "make things as right as possible" for everyone involved. That includes: repairing what has been broken, making society safer, attending to needs related to the behavior, and making amends.

In restorative justice, impact can have a ripple effect. The primary victims are those most impacted, including the people or institutions you've stolen from and your family members, who might have suffered from the consequences of your stealing (emotionally, financially, etc). Secondarily are others, such as the community.

Restorative justice is based on a concept of healing, which entails:

- Addressing the impact on others
- Addressing the needs of others
- Learning new behaviors to prevent relapse
- Restitution -- restoring or giving back

Case Example

John was referred to our program from his therapist. John was 45-years-old, had a law degree, and worked in a private law firm. He had a 20-year history of compulsive stealing behavior and spent his early time in group working on interventions so he could stop stealing. Later, after he stopped stealing, he began to ask himself what he should do with all the things he stole. Not only did these things trigger shameful feelings, but he also felt that he wanted all the stolen things out of his house. Most importantly, he felt he wanted to make reparations to his community. His therapist recommended that he thoughtfully consider his options and talk about his ideas in his group.

After a while John decided that the things that were still in good shape could be donated to a local homeless shelter. The other things, he tossed out, but decided to assess their value as though he'd purchased them. He talked about how his stealing was not about being unable to afford the things he stole, because he was well-off financially. After he assessed the value of the stolen items, he decided to make a contribution in that amount to a charity that worked with children. It was not a quick process because it took time as his therapist carefully worked with him to make sure he wasn't going to relapse while replacing the stolen items with purchased items. He made sure he was in regular contact with his therapist and his partner while he shopped. After he had made his "amends," he commented that getting support and help was the exact opposite of his previously secret and isolated life of stealing.

Exercises

1. What impact has your stealing behavior had on others? Who have been the primary victims, and the secondary? Write them all down *and* what the impact has been.

    <u>Primary Victims</u>

    <u>Secondary Victims</u>

2. What would restitution look like for you? Would you give money, return items, speak to a group about your experience, make a donation, or some combination? Think about the broader impact of your behaviors and how you might help to heal society/others.

3. Finally, write a letter making amends to those most impacted by your behavior. This letter / letters doesn't need to be mailed, but is very important that you write it/them. And be careful to take full responsibility for your behaviors – don't blame others or rationalize. Be heartfelt in your apology.

Chapter 14

Creating Healthy Intimacy and Relationships with Others

Relationships

To be in relationships with others is a basic human need. We all need to feel loved by others, love towards others, and feel connected to others.

People who get caught up in compulsive behaviors often feel very alone even when in committed relationships with others and/or with family. This is because hiding parts of yourself from others leads not only to depression and low self-worth, but also to loneliness. Additionally, core beliefs about self and others often lead to lack of relationships. In other words, the belief that "I'm unlovable" or that "people can't be trusted" also leads to feelings of isolation and loneliness/disconnection from others.

Relationship and Attachment

Relationship and attachment to others can be thought about in many different ways, for example, as in the following four relationship styles, or ways of forming attachments. In this model, everyone has a fundamental way they think about themselves and a fundamental way they think about others. These ways of thinking about yourself and others profoundly affect the way we form relationships and how we function once in a relationship.

1. **Secure**: A securely attached person has a positive sense of self and a positive sense of the other person. If they were to succinctly describe relationships it would sound like this: "I like myself and feel generally trusting and appreciative of others."

2. **Insecure-Preoccupied**: An insecure-preoccupied attachment is based on a negative sense of self, but a positive sense of other. It's also known as "insecure-wanting." In describing relationships, it would sound like this: "I don't like myself, and I long to be close to others and to be as good as them."

3. **Insecure-Dismissive**: An insecure-dismissive attachment is based on a positive sense of self, but a negative sense of other. This type of attachment is also known as "cold-avoidant." Describing this relationship would sound like: "I like myself, others can't be trusted."

4. **Insecure-Fearful**: An insecure-fearful attachment is based on a negative sense of self and a negative sense of the other. It is also known as "insecure-avoidant." It would sound like this: "I don't like myself and I don't trust anyone else either."

Of course, it should be noted that each of these exist on a continuum. In other words, we feel these things to a greater or lesser degree. But in our experience, people who compulsively steal have issues related to attachment, relationship and intimacy, and can usually place themselves in one of the insecure-based (#2, 3, or 4) relationship styles.

Why is this important? Because being aware of the way you form relationships and function in them is crucial. Having this insight can help you to understand why you have difficulty forming healthy, intimate, loving relationships with others. Addressing these core relationship beliefs and issues can help you learn how to form a different kind of relationship that will allow you to get your needs met in a deeper way.

Achieving Intimacy

Intimacy is being able to be yourself with another person and not having to pretend or play games. Intimacy is being genuinely close: truly knowing another person and being known by them. Intimacy is not the same thing as sex, and sex may or may not be intimate but may only *create the illusion* of closeness. Intimacy means opening up to someone, which means taking the risk of being rejected or hurt by them. **Intimacy means being vulnerable.**

Elements Necessary for Achieving Intimacy

1. **Recognizing who you are**: We can't be truly intimate with someone else until we're intimate with ourselves.

2. **Knowing yourself better**: It's crucial to know what you need, want and what you believe to be possible in a relationship.

3. **Accepting yourself** and **accepting imperfections in others**: These two go hand-in-hand. Often we are most critical of others when we are really unhappy with ourselves. It's essential that you learn to accept your own imperfections and to allow for others to have them as well.

4. **Developing trust and taking risks**: Creating an intimate relationship means that we have to be able to risk being vulnerable – to trust the other person with our emotions, thoughts and lives. The risk is we might get hurt in the process. Learning how to be intimate has to do with learning how to decide where boundaries and lines are, and how to trust, and how much to trust.

5. **Having healthy autonomy**: While it's crucial to learn how to depend on others in a healthy way, it's just as crucial for us to be able to be happy being alone, and to be able to function well outside of a relationship.

6. **Expressing affection**: Everyone needs affection. How this affection gets best expressed, and/or received, is best learned with the person in each relationship. The need is always there.

7. **Making a commitment**: Forming an intimate relationship involves commitment. The commitment is to the person, to the relationship and to the experience of everyone involved.

8. **Healthy communication**: As reviewed in earlier chapters, healthy communication is communication that takes work, knowledge, patience and sometimes risk. It's about taking responsibility for your own experience and being willing to hear and honor the experience of the other person – no matter how painful it may feel.

Case Example

Lorena was a 62-year-old professional woman referred by a community court. She'd been arrested for shoplifting and as dispensation of her case, she was asked to do community service and attend our program for treatment. She spent years as a psychiatric social worker and was deeply disturbed by her own "out-of-control" behaviors. She participated in group and individual therapy. She was a very friendly and kind woman, but found herself full of doubt, anger and anxiety with her individual therapist. Over the course of time, she realized that she was very worried that her therapist would be harshly critical of her. As a child her mother would frequently taunt and criticize her about her appearance, intelligence and her desire to learn new things and explore the world. Lorena came to understand that she had an insecure and fearful attachment with her mother, and frequently projected her anxiety of having the very same kind of relationship with her therapist.

It was a long and slow therapy. The therapist worked very gently and consistently to help Lorena realize that the therapeutic relationship with her was non-judgmental and that the therapist wanted to understand her and accept her fully. Over time, Lorena was able to relax and begin to work through the traumatic bonding with her mother and to learn to deal with her emotions and stop stealing. Lorena was eventually able to make fulfilling changes in her life that she never anticipated. She had always wanted to live by the ocean and eventually made that a reality. And she found a new relationship and a solid, happy partnership at the very young age of 65.

Exercises

1. What core – distorted – beliefs about relationship do you hold? Be as honest as you can. Imagine that you're talking with the person you trust the most, about what *you* believe about relationships. Listen to what you would say, and then write it down.

2. Identify your relationship style. Which describes you the best? If you could try a new style, which one would it be, and why?

3. Read through the elements necessary for achieving intimacy. Which of those elements do you feel you have/are doing, and which elements do you still need to work on? What is in the way of those elements that you don't have?

Chapter 15

Relapse Prevention I:

The "Cycle" revisited

Review of Important Terms/Concepts

- *Triggers*: External or internal situations, thoughts or feelings that can lead you to start thinking about stealing.
- *SUDs*: **Seemingly Unimportant Decisions** that lead you toward stealing without consciously recognizing you are headed in that direction.
- *Coping Strategy*: An alternative thought or behavior to those that lead you to steal. In other words, a new way to deal with difficult feelings and urges.

The Cycle of Stealing: putting the Cycle from Chapter 7 into use

Below is a review of the cycle that we wrote about in Chapter 7. At this point in the workbook you have gained enough knowledge about yourself so that you can re-visit this cycle and fill in the parts of it in a more complete way.

Being able to see this cycle clearly, and each of its components, forms the basis of your Relapse Prevention Plan. Once you can identify the parts of the process that lead to stealing, you will be able to (1) avoid situations, thoughts, fantasies and plans that lead to stealing, and (2) to learn how to take care of yourself and meet needs that arise – old triggers – in healthy and more fulfilling ways. Below is a review of the parts of the cycle you will be using to form a Relapse Prevention Plan:

1. *Situation/Lifestyle Risk Factors*: This is both the big picture and the small picture: what is happening in your life, and what is happening that day that leads to the urge to steal.
2. *Feelings & Triggers*: These are the feelings that automatically arise in response to a particular situation. Typically they are the uncomfortable ones that you try to avoid or feelings that create longing or desire.

3. *Fantasies*: These are fleeting images, ideas and/or memories which pop into the mind in response to feelings that have arisen. Sometimes they can become elaborate and lengthy.

4. *Thoughts*: These thoughts are efforts to re-evaluate the fantasies, to see if any of them would be practical solutions to the troublesome feelings that have arisen from the situation. For someone thinking clearly and truthfully, a good solution will be found. For someone caught in a pattern of thinking errors and patterns of negative behavior, the decision will not be a good one (i.e. to steal).

5. *Plan (and Seemingly Unimportant Decision)*: After the thinking evaluates the fantasies, a plan is made. Some plans are months in the making, some are weeks, some days and some only a moment before. Sometimes there isn't a full plan, just a little decision that puts you closer to stealing.

6. **High Risk Situation**: These are the situations that make you feel the most out of control, and are the most triggering of your stealing behavior.

7. **Loss of Control:** That point at which you "give up" and just steal something. Until this point, you've not stolen anything yet and even though it may feel "inevitable," you still have a choice *not* to steal.

8. **Action:** You steal something.

9. **Evaluation**: How you think about what happened, and then how you apply those thoughts about it in terms of the future.

What's hard about this?

- **Forming new coping strategies**: It's difficult to change course from a well-worn path. Even when we know that our actions don't really help us over the long term, the "quick fix," however temporary, is tempting. So finding new ways to cope is a challenge.

- **Acknowledging triggers**: This really has to do with becoming brutally honest with yourself, and is not easy. Part of why it's so challenging is because it ultimately entails giving things up that you might not want to do without.

- **Substance use & other potentially unhealthy behaviors**: Sometimes denial can mean that we want to see a particular behavior as just an isolated event and not connected to feelings and thoughts that prompt other unhealthy ways of coping: drinking, drug use, watching TV, internet surfing, eating, sex, or other behaviors.

- **Identifying feelings & needs**: Sometimes it can be a real challenge to identify what are the feelings and needs that underlie the automatic thoughts, fantasies and behaviors they prompt. And sometimes we can identify those feelings, but still feel very confused. We have to learn to tolerate that confusion until we can sort through it, rather than feeling like we need to act on it.

- **Slowing down**: Sometimes it feels like only a moment between situation and action. In relapse prevention, it's crucial to be able to slow down the process – delay the action – in order to be able to observe the feelings, thoughts, fantasies and planning. This is also necessary in order to make alternative choices.

Case Example - The Grocery List Intervention

Meredith was a 50-year-old social worker who had been stealing since she was 10. She'd grown up in a very poor family and hadn't been able to afford birthday presents, vacations or new clothes. As a child she remembered seeing her mom shoplift small things from the grocery store. Meredith was a very intelligent woman and had gone on to earn a Master's Degree and Ph.D. She was a highly sought after consultant working with the state government. She married an extremely successful criminal defense attorney and their net worth was in the millions. But Meredith stole from all kinds of stores. During her recovery she had the most difficult time stopping stealing from grocery stores. She realized that she stole items that her family never could afford when she was a child: imported cheese, pate and the more expensive food condiments. She could afford all the things she stole – and then some. Meredith had to make several important behavioral changes before and during her regular grocery store trips. Her treatment plan included the following:

1. She did as much of her shopping as possible via an online delivery service that one of the major grocery store chains provided.

2. When she went to stores, she never wore anything with pockets, no bulky clothes and she didn't carry a purse. She carried her wallet in one hand.

3. She always had a special list she and her therapist composed. At the top of the list she'd write something to remind her of the personal consequences of shoplifting. Then again in the middle of the list a different consequence reminder was added, and finally at the bottom of the list a last reminder. It looked something like this:

BEING ARRESTED WHEN I LEAVE THE STORE

GRAPES

MILK

BUTTER

CHEESE

HANDCUFFS

CHICKEN

PAPER TOWELS

BREAD

BAGELS

CALLING MY HUSBAND FROM JAIL AND ASKING FOR BAIL

Exercise – Forming a Relapse Prevention Plan

1. Complete the Cycle again, this time using everything you've learned from the previous chapters. Be as honest as you can about each step and include everything, even if you are uncertain.

My Cycle of Stealing

1. **Lifestyle Risk Factors:**

2. **Triggers:**

3. **Fantasy and Desire**:

4. **Plan** (and **Seemingly Unimportant Decision**):

5. **High Risk Situation:**

6. **Loss of Control:**

7. **Evaluation:**

2.   Make a list of new, alternative coping strategies.

3.   Make a list of triggers and things you may have to give up. Also include things you can't give up, but ways you might cope with them differently.

4.   What are some of the other unhealthy behaviors/coping strategies you employ?

5.   Which feelings and needs do you have a difficult time with? Brainstorm some alternative ways that you might deal with those feelings and meet the needs.

6.   Keep this plan where it is accessible to you and can be referred to when needed. Where might this be?

Chapter 16

Relapse Prevention II:

Lifestyle Inventory Journal and Concrete Next Step Plan

Stress – A Very Slippery Slope

- It's very important to take an honest look at your life and find out what is and is not working for you. When parts of your life are not working or are out of control, stress occurs. Stress, as you may know, can create physical and mental illness including depression and anxiety. As stress mounts, you become more impulsive, have a harder time resisting the urge to act-out (steal) and make poor choices. All of this can lead to a relapse.

- The Life Inventory gives you an opportunity to address each part of your life systematically – look at what is working and what isn't – and to prioritize what parts of your life you need to address/fix, so that you reduce the risk of stealing again over the long-term.

Life Inventory

- You'll be asked in the section below to think about each major area of your life. If a section does not apply, skip it and move on. You will be asked to do three things:

- Rate on a scale of 1 to 5 how well this part of your life is going: **1=Crisis, 2=Poor, 3=Erratic, 4=Adequate, 5=No improvement necessary**.

- Write about what is working and what is *not* working. Identify and name the problems and how you can improve these parts of your life.

- Rank each major life area according to which presents the most serious problem for you and creates the most stress in your life. This will allow you to complete the workbook with clear goals and action items to address in the next phase of your recovery work.

Journal Writing on the 17 Life Categories (some instruction on how to write a journal or about it)

- **YOUR STEALING:** How has it impacted your life, relationships and work? Do you have a criminal record? Do you have a felony? Do you still act-out? If so, where? When? How often? How much? Are you struggling to stop?

- **PHYSICAL HEALTH:** Are you taking care of your body? Do you exercise, eat right and get enough sleep? Do you have an illness or injury that makes taking care of yourself difficult? Do you have an eating disorder such as compulsive eating, sugar addiction, bulimia or anorexia? Do you have a body image problem? How do you feel about your body? Do you need to educate yourself about healthy eating habits, including nutrition, and exercise?

- **TRANSPORTATION:** Are you able to get from point A to point B without stress? Do you spend hours commuting? Have you lost your license due to an addiction? Do you experience road rage?

- **ENVIRONMENT:** Is your household disorganized, unkempt or chaotic? Is your house overly organized? Do you hoard? Do you deny yourself the things that would make your home function well? Do you get upset, obsessed or anxious if anything is out of place?

- **WORK:** Do you have work that is meaningful, fulfilling and meeting your financial needs? How are your professional relationships? Are you bored and longing for a career change? Do you need training, further education and professional development? Do you work too much or too little?

- **INTERESTS/HOBBIES/PASSIONS:** Do you have personal interests and hobbies? What are they? How much time do you spend on your interests? Are you able to pursue and participate in those interests on a regular basis? If you don't have any established interests, why not? What would it take to find something you like to do? Is money a problem? Do your partner, family and friends encourage you to pursue your interests?

- **SOCIAL LIFE:** Do you have a supportive network of friends and family? Do you know how to enjoy yourself with others? What do you like to do with your friends? Are you having any relationship problems with friends? Do you only do what your friends suggest, or do you ignore their suggestions? Do you isolate yourself?

- **INTIMATE PARTNER AND FAMILY:** Are you in a fulfilling relationship? Are you having any problems in your current relationship? Have you had a history of problems in this relationship or other relationships? How would you describe your relationships with your other family members? Do any of your relationships need improvement in communication or better boundaries?

- **FINANCES:** Are you living in financial reality? Are you educated about your finances and understand how to earn, save and invest for your goals and your future? Are you having financial problems? Do you overspend or in debt? Or does your partner overspend or incur debt?

- **SEX LIFE:** Is your sexual life fulfilling? Are you sexually frustrated, compulsive or unable to enjoy sex? Do you have any history of sexual trauma such as rape, molestation or incest? Do you have a history of sexual addiction or acting sexually compulsive? Have you sought support for these issues?

- **CHANGE, TRANSITIONS AND LOSS:** How do you feel about change? Are you currently dealing with a transition or loss? How do you handle change? Does change make you anxious? Do you know how to accept loss? Do you let yourself grieve?

- **COMMUNICATION:** What is your communication style? Do you confront problems or issues directly? Do you avoid conflict or withdraw when you are uncomfortable? Do you have difficulty listening or paying attention? Do you anger easily? Do you know how to talk about your feelings and problems with others?

- **SPIRITUALITY & MEANING:** Do you have a religious or spiritual practice that brings your life meaning? Do you feel this lacking in your life? If you are agnostic or atheist, what brings meaning to your life? Have you ever experienced judgment, criticism or abuse by a religious leader, institution or member?

- **MENTAL HEALTH:** Do you suffer from a mood disorder or other psychiatric problem? If so, have you received treatment? Has the treatment been successful? If not, what are you currently doing to address these problems?

- **OTHER ADDICTIONS:** Do you use alcohol or drugs? Do you gamble, shop or have other impulsive or compulsive behaviors? Have you ever evaluated these behaviors or had professional evaluations? Have you ever been in treatment? Are you in 12-step recovery for another impulse control disorder and if so, how is it going?

- **PARENTING or CARE-GIVING:** Do you have children? What are the joys? What are the challenges? Do you feel overwhelmed, or do you feel that you have enough support, information and help? Do any of your children have special needs and challenges? Do you care for an aging or ill relative or partner? How much time, money and energy does this situation ask from you?

- **FEELINGS:** Are you able to feel your feelings and name them? Do you connect with your inner life? Do you ever feel overwhelmed and unable to manage all your feelings? Do you feel numb and withdraw frequently? Do you anger easily and not understand why? Are you afraid of your feelings? Which ones? Do you feel like your feelings are not understood by yourself or others?

Ranking the 17 on a 1-5 scale   Rank

- Your Impulse Control Disorder
- Physical Health
- Transportation
- Environment
- Work
- Interests/Hobbies/Passions
- Social Life
- Intimate Partner/Family
- Finances
- Sex Life
- Change/Transitions/Loss
- Communication
- Spirituality/Meaning
- Mental Health/Mood
- Other Addictions
- Parenting/Care-giving
- Feelings

Totals

- Count up and list the 1's

- Count up and list the 2's

- Count up and list the 3's

- Count up and list the 4's

- Count up and list the 5's

Concrete Action Plan

- You can, for the moment, cross-off and ignore the 5's and 4's as areas of your life that are not causing you significant stress. But please review these areas on a monthly basis to make sure there haven't been any significant changes in terms of increased stress.
- Now with each of the following categories starting with the 1's then 2's and finally 3's, put them in order of rank from most stressful to least.

- Ranked 1's

- Ranked 2's

- Ranked 3's

- Your 1's and 2's need to be immediately acknowledged, addressed and discussed in your individual therapy, on-going group therapy and any 12-step programs you attend. Your 3's need to be monitored on a monthly basis and planned for realistically. Your therapist and recovering group members will be giving you feedback on your plan.

Congratulations! You are on your way to a life free from compulsive stealing.

Appendix A

Compulsive Stealing and the Holidays

The holiday season comes with expectations and hopes of warmth, laughter and closeness with friends and family. And yet at the same time, more people are tempted to shoplift and are arrested for shoplifting during the Christmas holiday season than at any other time of the year. Here are just a few reasons:

- Spending more time in stores
- Feeling pressured to get gifts
- Financial worry and stress due to increase spending at holidays
- More store security presence in stores
- More store clerks and associates working
- Family stress due to holiday commitments and expectations
- Unhappy and painful memories of losses during holidays
- Unrealistic expectations of self and others during holidays
- More alcohol consumption, which reduces inhibitions and increases impulsive actions.

There are greater time, family, social, professional and financial demands at this time of year. As a result, most of us feel an increase of stress. That increase of stress is particularly challenging for those with impulse control disorders which are made worse by increased stress: **the ability to resist impulses rests on the ability to decrease stress in one's life.**

So, this is a time to be aware of that stress and make the necessary changes to insure that you won't have a shoplifting slip or relapse. Here are a few suggestions for getting through the holiday season without a stealing incident:

- Make a list of people to whom you plan to give gifts – and stick to it.
- Create a realistic budget that won't leave you financially stressed.

- Can you do your shopping through catalogs or online?
- Create a list of gifts – write it down – and include reminders that keep you mindful of the consequences of stealing such as handcuffs, police, bail or jail. Keep that list in one hand as you are shopping.
- Don't browse or linger in stores.
- Ask for help if you can't find something in order to stop yourself from spending too much time in the store.
- Shop with a trusted family member or friend.
- Make some of your gifts.
- Be honest with yourself and others. If you can't afford to buy gifts or go to events, there's no shame in keeping your feet planted squarely in reality!
- Volunteer at a local organization and let others know that your gift for them is a few hours of time in their honor.
- Talk in your support groups, with trusted friends, with trusted family or in therapy, about your feelings about the holidays and gift giving.
- Reach out for professional help.
- Commit not to steal gifts – you need to keep yourself safe.
- You can ride out the urge to steal. Make yourself a cup of tea, take a bath, call a friend, go for a walk, do something to help you relax – the craving and urge will pass.
- Remember, most family members and friends would not want to receive a stolen gift. If a family member or friend is OK with you risking your safety to give them something, then you are in a destructive and likely co-dependent relationship, and they are enabling your stealing, and you are enabling an unhealthy relationship pattern. Get professional help to break the harmful cycle.

You, your recovery, and your safety are so much more important than "giving" that which you don't have, want or need to give. The most important gift you can give to yourself and to those who love you is the maintenance of your sobriety and your recovery from stealing. So try to remember that this time of year is traditionally a time to turn inward, reflect, rest and renew yourself.

References

American Psychiatric Association. (2000). *Diagnostic and statistical manual of mental disorders* (4th ed., text rev.). Washington, DC: Author.

Bartholomew, K., & Horowitz, L. M. (1991). Attachment styles among young adults: A test of a four-category model. *Journal of Personality and Social Psychology, 61*, 226-244.

Claassen, R. (1996). Restorative Justice – Fundamental Principles. *Center for Peacemaking and Conflict Studies, Fresno Pacific College.*

Cool Down: Anger and How to Deal with It. (2008) The Mental Health Foundation; London, England.

Grant, Jon, MD., Kim, S.W., Fricchione, G. (2004) *Stop Me Because I Can't Stop Myself: Taking Control of Impulsive Behavior.* McGraw-Hill.

Jentsch, J.D., Taylor J.R. (1999) Impulsivity resulting from frontostriatal dysfunction in drug abuse: implications for the control of behavior by reward-related stimuli. Psychopharmacology (Berl), 146: 373-390.

McElroy, S., Hudson, S., Pope, H., Keck, P., & Aizley, H. The DSM-III-R impulse control disorders not elsewhere classified: Clinical characteristics and relationships to other psychiatric disorders. American Journal of Psychiatry, 149, 318-327.

Morin, J. & Levenson, J. (2002). *The Road to Freedom.* Oklahoma City, Oklahoma: Wood 'N' Barns Publishing & Distribution.
O'Boyle, M and Barratt, E.S.(1993) Impulsivity and DSM-III-R personality disorders. Personality and Individual Differences, 14, 609-611.

Prochaska, J. O. and C. C. DiClemente (1992). *Stages of Change in the Modification of Problem Behaviors.* Newbury Park, CA, Sage.

Willcut, E.G., Pennington, B.F., Chhabildas, N.A., Friedman, M.C., Alexander,J.(1999) Psychiatric morbidity associated with DSM IV ADHD in a non-referred sample of twins. Journal of American Academy of Child and Adolescent Psychiatry, 38, 1355-1362.

Offense Chain. Courtesy of Charles Flinton, Ph.D. (2006)

Grocery Store List. Courtesy of Jon Grant, MD

Acknowledgements

This workbook is the culmination of many years of experience and exchange of ideas. We would like to acknowledge and appreciate the staff at the Pathways Institute for contributing to this effort through their willingness to learn, share, contribute their thoughts and experiences, and grow with us. Thank you also to Dan Dippery and Michael Nold, for your thorough and thoughtful editing.

We acknowledge and appreciate the experiences, perspectives, and hard work of those we have worked with over the years who struggle with compulsive stealing. Your commitment to treatment and recovery in spite of how painful and difficult it can be, has been the inspiration for this project.

With this workbook, we hope to reach the wider community of mental health professionals. Kleptomania and compulsive stealing are grossly under-researched and there are few therapists with the expertise necessary to effectively treat this problem. We hope this workbook inspires you to join us and enrich the thinking and clinical work in this much needed area of mental health and community safety.

To all victims of those who steal compulsively and family members who have loved ones who suffer from this disorder: we know that our endeavor cannot erase your loss. We only hope that it will help to make society safer and help restore what has been stolen.

Finally, we would like to acknowledge our families. Thank you for your patience and support as we have worked to create a program that provides new pathways for those who desperately need it.

About Pathways Institute for Impulse Control

The Pathways Institute provides the highest standards of assessment and evidenced-based treatment to those (adults, couples, families, adolescents, and children) suffering from the devastating effects of impulse control disorders, addictions, out-of-control behaviors, and/or learning differences. We provide a compassionate, non-judgmental and safe environment so patients can explore the origins and meanings of their behaviors and make necessary changes to stop these behaviors and prevent future relapse.

At Pathways Institute, we believe we are all entitled to live in a safe community, one in which individuals can create meaningful lives and make contributions to our community's health, well-being and future. There are no "quick fixes" for the conditions we address. But we offer patients and the criminal justice system accurate risk assessment, court testimony and alternatives to incarceration. We provide this opportunity through behavior containment and intervention with repeat offenders who are overwhelming the courts and/or facing loss of livelihood and relationships.

We are a team of inter-disciplinary, licensed mental health professionals and associates, who provide cutting-edge care: through our extensive experience, through on-going education, training, research and on-going relationships with experts in the field. It is also our goal to transmit our knowledge and experience to other therapists so they can learn to effectively assess and treat these populations, and so they may provide the most effective treatment both while in our employment and if/when they operate independently.

For more information on Pathways Institute resources, please go to the website **www.pathwaysinstitute.net** or call **415.267.6916** for information on treatment, materials for licensing, workbooks, workshops, and training.

About the Authors

Pathways Institute for Impulse Control was founded by Elizabeth Corsale, M.A., MFT, and Samantha Smithstein, Psy.D.:

Elizabeth Corsale, M.A., MFT

Ms. Corsale is a licensed Marriage and Family Therapist. She has worked for over 18 years with individual, couples, and families, on issues related to trauma, attachment, and relationships, learning and attention differences, and has specialized in impulsive disorders and addictions. She has offered comprehensive education, training, outreach and consultation to clinical professionals and to criminal justice institutions. She also founded and directed one of the few nationally recognized treatment programs for compulsive stealing: the Shoplifters Recovery Treatment Program (SRTP) – now a part of Pathways Institute. She is a Certified Problem Stealing Therapist (CPST) and trainer, and is a member of the California Association of Marriage and Family Therapists (CAMFT) and the Parents Education Network (PEN). She also provides treatment in her private practice. (MFC 36769)

Samantha Smithstein, Psy.D.

Dr. Smithstein is a licensed Clinical and Forensic Psychologist who has assessed and provided help for adults, adolescents, couples and children for over 15 years on issues related to relationships, attachment, trauma, addiction, and impulse control. Dr. Smithstein also has considerable experience related to sexuality, working with and evaluating people who have a sexual addiction and/or have been arrested, charged, convicted or otherwise gotten into trouble for their sexual behaviors. As a forensic psychologist, she has provided hundreds of evaluations for the courts and has provided expert court testimony and community consultation and training. She is a member of the American Psychological Association (APA), Association for Treatment of Sexual Abusers (ATSA), and the California Coalition On Sexual Offending (CCOSO). She is a Certified Problem Stealing Therapist (CPST). She also provides treatment in her private practice. (PSY19074)

Made in the USA
San Bernardino, CA
29 August 2016